1965, I was 15. The Lehigh , and Lafaye great opportunities to gig. Most of these "Animal House." One, however, was our rite of passage. Booked to play at Lafayette,the agent "forgot" to tell us we were going to back up a striking, wailing black female singer, Queenie Lyons, former backup singer for James Brown! For one bluesy, soulful night, The Limits became Queenie Lyons' CUBS!

1971, I'm 21. WAX, our Philadelphia band, enters the prestigious Record Plant in NYC to begin our first major label album. We are in the small room, on either side The Who, and John Lennon! What are WE doing here?? Its heady, high, creative, and mind-blowing. 4 weeks later it comes crashing down. We are locked out of the studio. The label is shut down by the IRS. Have we hit rock bottom?

Mid 90s..in Atlanta, we were doing a soundcheck at the huge Georgia Dome for a big oldies show. The Techniques were backing several artists, and jamming to get the right sound. I heard another guitarist playing. I looked over and saw JAMES BURTON..Elvis' guitarist, Ricky Nelson's guitarist..and Jerry Lee Lewis' guitarist..I froze..feeling inadequate..in the presence of a genius. James just smiled and said, "Keep jamming!" We played for some twenty minutes. When he said I, and the band played really well, I felt as if I'd arrived. Several years later, after a casino show in Shreveport with Tommy Roe, we all headed to James Burton's club and jammed until the wee hours.

2014 I receive the Pennsylvania Governor's Lifetime Achievement Award in Music, and the Lehigh Valley Music Award's Lifetime Achievement.

2018 The BOX TOPS are inducted into the Memphis Music Hall of Fame.

READ ON AND JOIN THE JOURNEY!

High
in the
Mid-'6os

How to Have a Fabulous Life in Music without Being Famous

by Rick Levy

Heartfelt Dedication

To my mom, Myra Levy. She was the ultimate peacemaker and harmonizer, nurtured feelings of self-worth and esteem, was loving to everyone, and understood me without the need for words.

To my dad, Mort Levy. He was compassionate, generous, and strong beyond my comprehension, and always with unbelievable humility and silence. Without his lifelong support on all levels, I could never have attempted to follow my dreams. He said, "When they spit in your face, pretend it's rain." He taught me to build bridges, not burn them.

To my son, Jonah Levy. My best friend, and to quote Blood Sweat and Tears' first album, "child is father to the man," Jonah helped me become a true man, and together we continue to grow in mutual love, respect, innocence, awe, and friendship.

To my first love. Candy Hunt, who dazzled my heart with the infinite value of love at a young age where there are no boundaries to possibility.

To Carlie. Crazy love…heartbreak…and an amazing son together…thank you!

To Leiza. I was middle aged, and your honesty and insight made us best friends and soulmates. That has never faltered, even though we are no longer together.

To my brothers in music, The Limits, WAX, and all the rockers with whom I have shared the rehearsal spaces, stages, and the road. We do what most people only wish!

Thank you, all.

Acknowledgements

I would like to thank attorneys Lloyd Remick and Helen Richardson for a lifetime of friendship, advice, and putting up with my endless questions and ideas. You have made my career and personal life more enjoyable.

I also wish to thank Peggy Salvatore, a great singer and editor, who made my written journey into something more readable, and, I think, powerful.

AN INVITATION TO ENJOY

by Lloyd Zane Remick Esq.

So, travel back with me half a century when I, as a young entertainment lawyer, am introduced to a group of young rock and rollers from the University of Pennsylvania in Philadelphia, from which I graduated. The group, with long hair, paisley shirts and bellbottoms were a far cry from when I attended Penn, wearing three piece suits and white bucks. The group was "WAX", and ironically was really good..not celebrity great, but good, and successful in the Philadelphia market and almost nationally. Most of the members went on to successful careers (never iconic) in the music business, from producing to writing to performing.

In the hundreds, probably thousands of musicians I have seen....many try to "make it" while maintaining full time jobs, working on their music on the side. Not so Rick Levy. He once told me music was a common denominator for all people and he loved creating and performing music and it was his life's work regardless of the degree of celebrity status he attained. Who knew that 50 years later, through a friendship and professional relationship, he would still be at it, loving it much as when he first started.

Rick's memoir and journey for the last 50 years gives readers a true insight into his life and the life of musicians who never quite obtained celebrity status...but still plow on, playing and "gigging" as their life's work. Rick has experienced it all as a performer, recording artist, writer, publisher, agent, manager, and touring musician. This book is a MUST READ to really understand the trials and tribulations and success of someone who loves his craft. "High in the Mid 60's" is a nonstop readers' must.

Lloyd Zane Remick is a well known entertainment lawyer and manager for over 50 years, and the author of a legal crime novel, Two Times Platinum, that exposes the seedy side of the music and sports world, and how deals really get done.

Foreword

Let me start by telling you what this book is not. This book is not going to be one of those pathetically inane, VH1-type "Behind the Music" episodes...humble beginnings.... superstardom.... drugs and alcohol to within minutes of extinction... revelation, resurrection, reclamation...ending with a comeback that nobody cares about.

That story has been told and retold. It is not my story, though. Since I never officially made it in those terms, this story may actually resonate with average people. There's no comeback to care about, because I haven't gone away, and I haven't arrived either.

Maybe my brain just needs to clean out, or maybe because I live a life I love, and numerous people have asked me to try and trace the path, I think I do need to find out just why and how music—specifically rock, pop, soul, and blues—has become my pole star in a bizarre and chaotic world. Any kid who ever played "Louie, Louie," "Gloria," "Woolly Bully," "Twist and Shout," and countless other garage band gems knows the transcendent moments that are as close to enlightenment as it comes. That I've been able to spend most of my life in this zone is truly amazing.

So, to paraphrase Mick Jagger, please allow me to introduce myself.

Rick Levy
August 2018

Chapter 1: Cardboard Sideburns

November 1, 1949

Scorpio, Scorpio rising

Actually, I have very few recollections of my childhood. I have to think really, really, really hard to conjure any images or memories. I think this is odd because my parents were absolutely loving, giving, supportive, and kind. I had the kind of childhood people want to remember.

Mom, Myra Demchick Levy, and I were always in tune and close. Dad, Mort "the Sport" Levy, was a kind and honorable gentleman, and with every passing year I realize he really was a giant of a man. My older sister, Judi, was my first music partner in a folk duo. I'm told I was the recipient of more than one black eye resulting from sibling play/warfare. We were a pretty wholesome, loving family living in Allentown, PA.

So, unless I was molested by some foul-smelling relative, or some such unmentionable disaster, I don't know why my BM (Before Music) life is a mystery. I've spoken to Alex Chilton[1] about this as he said most of his early childhood is devoid of memories, as well. Alex, for those who don't know, was the lead singer of the 60's hit group, The Box Tops, and consequently, of Big Star. He thinks because his youth was so utterly placid and happy, there wasn't much to make the brain develop to have memories. I don't know if that's sound science, but it seems to ring true to me. I have, however, successfully squeezed a few morsels from childhood, and perhaps they shed some light on my "rock climb".

1   Alex Chilton passed away in 2010

My most vivid memory finds me sitting on a tall lifeguard stand in Atlantic City, New Jersey. I was maybe 4 years old, watching my folks swim in the ocean, bathed in moonlight. As long as I can remember, I have wanted to live by the ocean. I do now, and maybe that seed was planted back then "Under the Boardwalk."

Yes, apparently, I always had problems submitting to authority. I fought the law. I ran away from 1st grade and hid behind the West End Pharmacy. I even was asked to leave the Cub Scouts because I forged my dad's name on some merit badge achievement test involving knots or some such nonsense.

My earliest memories are few, but they are vivid and definitely foreshadowed the soul of, if not a rock musician, certainly one of a free spirit.

The most crystalline moment of my childhood moment, however, was prescient. My "Uncle" Elliot presented me with the first Elvis Presley album. Shortly after that, at six or seven, I was running around the house having glued cardboard sideburns to my face. My first epiphany.

The psychiatrists among you will have fun with this, but I am embarrassed to admit that a few years later I set a fire in our new house. I couldn't have been more than nine or ten, and probably suffering from pre-adolescent esteem issues. My plan was to start a small fire…be the first to smell smoke…call the fire department…and BE A HERO! Everything went according to plan until my dad looked me in the eyes, and I started to bawl, admitting the whole thing! In the end, I guess I was punished, but still assured that I was valued and loved. Just that one act of parental wisdom is why it is no wonder that to this day I cringe at the sight or report of parental violence toward children.

Ford and Friends in West Allentown

Fred Fraenkel, Bob Holtz, Steve Kaplan, Doug Barolsky, Ron Krull, Ron Wolfe, Steve Cohen and I consumed quantities of Yocco's hot dogs and chocolate milk in our adolescence. Yocco's is an Allentown tradition started by the Iacocca family. Yes, that same family who produced Lee Iacocca who rose to lead the Ford Motor Co.'s development of the iconic Mustang and later, the Pinto. The Mustang means he can be forgiven the Pinto. Later, Lee Iacocca rose to national attention when he led Chrysler out of bankruptcy. Before the Mustang, there were Yocco's hot dogs. Their digestive effect was far superior to any new age high colonic cleansing treatment. Perhaps this regimen led me to my long-time vegetarian lifestyle.

Well, that's really about it. I don't have many detailed tidbits of my youth, but I do see some patterns that stirred my soul and loins even at a tender age. Maybe the rest of the journey is unnecessary, but I'm on a roll now.

Oh, wait! Before we leave my tender years, I figured it out! I was sent to eight-week overnight camp when I was only four-and-a-half-years old. Cruel and unreasonable, you say? Maybe, but then again there was a kid named Maxie Weinberg in my bunk...Maxie Weinberg...could he have been *that* Max Weinberg?...Springsteen's future drummer???

My Guardian Angel

Elliot Wexler, or Uncle Elliot to me, is truly my guardian angel. He was, I am convinced, the main reason why I still love to play a very loud "E" chord.

Elliot was my father's college football teammate and roommate at the University of Pennsylvania. He was so close to our family that the title "uncle" just seemed perfect. I had written this section on Uncle Elliot, and frankly thought it was pretty complete. When I showed it to my then agent, Bob Fleck, he suggested I really dig and discover just how this one man completely set my life course in motion. So, I am sitting here a few days after the devastation of Hurricane Katrina in 2005 trying to let go of the present and relive the sensations that were such primal forces in my life.

Elliot worked in the mystical, magical, unexplainable record business in New York City. During his career he worked with the Decca, London, and Columbia labels. As far as I know, he discovered a very young Buddy Greco, the noted jazz vocalist/pianist, in Philadelphia. My dad told me that Elliot took the young, pimply, inexperienced Greco under his wing. In New York, Buddy's appearance was enhanced and his professionalism developed. Uncle Elliot was responsible for all this.

Uncle Elliott also served as personal assistant to the great Benny Goodman. Now that *is* something! Of course, as a kid living in Allentown, PA, I knew nothing of this. I just knew he was a bachelor with a cool Manhattan apartment. Amazingly, while I cannot remember what my own childhood house looked like, I vividly recall his swinging New York apartment, complete with stacks of wax, a grimy kitchen, and a great balcony overlooking Manny Wolfe's restaurant on Forty-ninth Street. He also had an original Wurlitzer electric piano in the living room...just like Ray Charles played on "What'd I Say"!

You see, I was a typical middle class, overprotected kid. I wasn't spoiled, but we really never lacked for comforts either. Life was quite by the book and governed by orderliness, education and routines. So, it was quite surprising that while I would not be permitted to wander far from the neighborhood, my folks would happily put me on a bus alone to travel to New York City to spend a great weekend with Uncle Elliot.

His life seemed so phenomenal, liberating, and exciting. What I didn't know was that he never smoked or drank, and was, by all accounts, a very quiet, reserved gentleman. To me, he was a cool, handsome man on the phone talking to artists, A&R men, radio DJ's, TV people, and it was so fucking slick! There were no dress codes, no timeclocks, no bosses looking over his shoulder. Again, I realized none of this consciously as a youngster, but am quite sure my own rebellious desire to be my own boss and survive in the music business was nurtured by these experiences. Truthfully, I don't even know if Uncle Elliot was financially successful. I just was totally turned on and enthralled by the music and the muse.

Life really did change from black-and-white to Technicolor when Uncle Elliot showed up at our house in Allentown, bringing Elvis' first LP. This was 1956, and I was seven years old.

The aforementioned sideburn epiphany happened as I ran around pretending to play guitar. A few years later, Uncle Elliot would give me both a record player and tape recorder. As a young teen, I wore out my copy of The Rolling Stones' "Out of Our Heads" album, playing along with every track, every night.

Uncle Elliot also found the first song for The Limits to record in 1965. Turns out that "Say It Again" was written by the great P.F. Sloan of the Grassroots. It was covered by an Aussie group, Ray Brown and the Whispers. The innocent young Limits lads loved the tune and recorded it. Not a bad find for a fledgling group.

Sadly, Uncle Elliot died of cancer in 1966, just as my unpredictable trip through the music business was getting started. There is absolutely no doubt in my mind that listening to music in his apartment, going to swanky and not so swanky eateries, and taking in the excitement and prana of his life put the music business bug in me. While most kids don't even have a spark of passion at an early age, I had a huge inferno burning—not just for the music, but for the entire business and lifestyle.

To this day, Uncle Elliot's picture is by my bedside, and I do talk to him almost daily.

Stewball, Shaved Head, Bar Mitzvah and Bomb Shelter

I'm still not quite sure what Puff the Magic Dragon is about. It's just a kids' tune, right?

But at thirteen, I wore a black roll neck sweater and played my first Martin guitar, a nylon string classic folk guitar, accompanying my sister, Judi. Judi was three years older than me, and she and I would harmonize on "Where Have All the Flowers Gone," "Stewball," "Tom Dooley," and other folk favorites. We were very clean, and most importantly, we were *soft*. We could even perform a few ditties for our parents' dinner parties.

While our duet was going on, I convinced my mom to drive me to the bad section of Allentown for a weekly guitar lesson with a genius. Always dressed in black, with a shaved head, Watts Clark chained smoked Camels. I am not sure how he ended up in Allentown, but he played all over the country in big bands and jazz ensembles. He lived in a dark, ominous apartment, and delicately conjured angels when he played his D'Angelico guitar. Not only did he teach technical and theoretical skills, but he embodied a musician—easy-going but focused, timeless yet reckless, and totally magnetic. It took me years to process the rhythmic knowledge he imparted, and I am still unlocking aural dimensions.

The chord scales he taught me—ones I didn't even realize what I was playing—have become a lauded style of my rock and soul playing. Shit. He was just so cool! That's the way I wanted to be, but of course, I also had to study for my Bar Mitzvah.

The Torah lessons got a bit sidetracked by the Cuban Missile Crisis, which culminated with the Soviet Union backing down on Oct 22, 1962. Even so, millions of Americans were convinced they were going to be incinerated and radiated by the Red Menace. I did celebrate my Bar Mitzvah in November of '62, but meanwhile my enterprising father was plotting a new business venture.

Certain that middle class Americans would want protection from impending doom, Mort and a close friend and business associate decided they would go into the "Bomb Shelter" business. I find this hilarious, as there were no standards for protection...how deep...how thick...how long does one even stay in the shelter? Even more zany, dad and his partner made a bet of some kind, and the LOSER had to have the prototype built at HIS home! WE LOST!

Early in 1963, the bulldozer, backhoe, and cement trucks arrived and a concrete tomb, three feet below the basement, with walls three feet thick, was built. It was so surreal. At the back end of the basement, we would go down several steps and come upon silver-painted, steel, stable-type doors complete with a sliding "speakeasy" peephole to see if half-eaten-away survivors were trying to get in. Now there was not even a seal around the doors anyway, so I'm guessing we would not have been spared the contamination. The shelter was probably 12 x 8 feet. There were four Spartan cots that folded against the bare white concrete walls. They'd release on chains, and we were supposed to sleep on these! Shelves were stocked with a 2-week supply of food, water, and medicine. WHO knew if 2 weeks was long enough?

The *coup de grace*, however, was the little chemical toilet hidden behind a plastic shower curtain. I'm convulsing with laughter now just thinking about doing our business behind a shower curtain. My dad was never quiet! Oh, but…we're not done yet. How were we to breathe? A crank handled intake fan was supposed to bring air into the shelter. Again, "the experts" said the filter would keep out radiation and contaminants.

If this wasn't insane enough, for months my dad held periodic drills where we'd all be timed getting down into the shelter. We'd check the Geiger counter, food supplies, and the dreaded chemical toilet. My sister and I finally told them we'd rather die than stay down there for two weeks. When my sister and I were preparing to sell the house after my father passed, we opened up the secret panel that was bolted shut for 45 years. There was actually a firearm. We don't know if that was for intruders or us…if the world had indeed ended!

The business venture failed miserably and not one other shelter was built. Ours became a cold, dank refuge for bugs, spiders and all sorts of mold and other creatures. The only saving grace was that during my college years, I'd bring friends home and we'd go the bomb shelter to get high! The filter intake fan worked too!! Back in the day I thought about sneaking girls down there, but that was just way too creepy. As our collective fear of imminent nuclear death has diminished, it was a fitting end that when the house was sold, the new owners turned the bomb shelter into a wine cellar!

My long-time friend, and editing consultant, Peggy Salvatore, reflected on some of the lifelong effects of growing up at this time. "I think it affected our mindset and the way we saw the world. We lived in the face of death, and because of that it influenced our music and probably was partially behind the drug culture. We had a sense that life was senseless, that we wouldn't live a full life and we didn't have control of a future we might not (even) have. Peace, love and rock 'n roll. Sex, drugs and rock 'n roll…it all ended in rock 'n roll. We had songs like *Where Have all the Flowers Gone?*, *Live for Today*, and *Eve of*

Destruction. Well, here we still are, rockin' and rollin'!"

Outcasts

Nobody is named Irwin Goldberg. Certainly not a kid in school. Still, there he was, a classically trained pianist, record collector, audiophile, and rock n roll nut. Later, we would introduce him on stage as Steve Gold.

I met Irwin at Opportunity School. Irwin swears that his earliest memory of me consists of Dick Gutman, the wooden block dropper, and myself ruthlessly making fun of everyone. Maybe Dick dropped blocks on both our heads. Why else would we have been such assholes? We had to talk or run our way out of more than one fight with jocks and vo-techies in high school.

Irwin also recalled my mom's way-cool 1958 yellow Ford convertible. She was so far ahead of her time. In Allentown, a group of students was identified as "mentally superior"—HAH! They even put that stamp on our report cards. We were bused to Jefferson Elementary School and had so-called advanced courses. Who knows about the pros and cons of this concept, but I did learn Typing and Spanish starting in third grade. *Ahora puedo hablar espanol,* and I can still type 50 words per minute!

In the fall of 1964, Irwin and I were in tenth grade at William Allen High School where we met Randy Cohen. Two years older, Randy was so cool with long curly hair, a Lambretta motor scooter, and Bob Dylan records. The Outcasts were born with the addition of Mike Mittman on rhythm guitar, and believe it or not, a female bass player. She was not quite a babe, one could open a beer can with her buck tooth, but it was pretty far out being the only garage band in town with a chick. Mike's dad supplied popcorn and confections to local movie theaters. Irwin played this rare Hammond Extravoice organ, and I was really proud of my Kent guitar! I do remember unloading Irwin's organ from a truck filled with bags of movie popcorn. I guess it made good padding, anyway.

The Outcasts' career lasted exactly three gigs—two at the YMCA and one at the Jewish Community Center. We grossed a total of 72 dollars, and during a break at the final 'Y' show, some idiot stepped on Mike's beautiful Gibson guitar. All in all, it was a losing, albeit fun, operation. Randy has gone on to become a highly successful journalist, and Mike is a well-known DJ and sports announcer.

Sadly, no recordings exist of this early musical incarnation.

Chapter 2

STIMIL Spelled Backwards

"Guys, the name The Limits stinks...it'll have to go."
"No Billy, you'll have to go!"

So, the mysterious Billy Stimil exited the newly formed Limits, never to be heard from again. I never met Billy Stimil, but the guys tell me he was in the band for about one week playing keyboards.

They came up with the name The Limits after jamming on the instrumental tune, "Out of Limits." Billy didn't like the name, and the guys didn't like Billy. To this day I cannot fathom the karma and irony behind his exit and my entrance and yes... it's true...Stimil spelled backwards is Limits!

Thus, The Limits were born in 1964. I was not involved at the time. The band consisted of Jack Shaffer (drums), Chris Jones (guitar), and Pat McGinley[2] (guitar, vocals.) Chris' older brother, Beau, played bass and sang when he was not away at prep school. I knew Jack, and in March of 1965 I auditioned for the band. My audition consisted of Chris calling Beau on the phone at the Hill School (where Beau's classmate was one Oliver Stone, the legendary movie producer, director and screenwriter) in Pottstown, Pa. Chris said that I could play lead guitar, but first Beau wanted to hear for himself, so I proceeded to play some rudimentary Chuck Berry licks over the phone and landed a spot. Little did I know that soon I'd be running the show.

Thus, my lifelong friendship with the Jones family began, and continues to this day.

Their father, Alvin Jones, was a *bona fide* WWII hero at

2   Sadly, Pat passed away in August of 2005.

the Battle of the Bulge and became a principal in Jones Motor Company after the war. He was also a shrewd investor, retiring at fifty to a very comfortable life. Jean Jones, his wife, became my second mom during the early Limits' years. Very proper, well-mannered, intelligent, and loving, she welcomed rehearsals, parties, more rehearsals and still more parties with saintly patience and graciousness.

The Jones boys (Beau, Rook, and Chris...god, I love those guys) are as different from one another as one can possibly imagine. John (Beau) Jones is the oldest and three years older than me. He straddled the line between genius and madman. An amazing, naturally gifted musician, he voraciously collected "stuff," and was a true philosopher and spiritualist. He was so spaced and flexible that during our later years in yet another band, the Philadelphia band Wax, he continued full-time military duty at a secure missile base and played bass for arguably the most popular and busiest original band in Philly. Much, much more on the Beau connection to follow but for now, suffice to say Beau's son, Spencer, plays violin, bass, and guitar, and has his own rock band today.

Middle brother Richard (Rook) Jones is one year older than me and was the original Limits' lead singer. Rook, honestly, was a fair singer, but then none of us was outstanding. We did, however, work our asses off learning harmonies, and vocals became a Limits' trademark. Rook was a great front man. Bedecked in the latest Mod or Psychedelic fashions, he pranced onstage and was a formidable chick magnet. I am not sure Rookie ever saw the band as the all-encompassing, life-changing experience that I did, but then again, he does still own his original leopard skin vest! Today, Cliff, one of Rook's sons, is in his own rock band.

Chris Jones, the baby in the band and the family, had, and still has, an uncanny ability to cop licks off records. He's a fine guitarist, and excellent pedal steel guitarist. He seemed to easily add very tasty guitar fills to the Limits' sound, and I think he could have succeeded in Nashville as a steel guitarist had he driven himself.

In March, 1965, The Limits were ready to take on the music

world. Somehow, The Limits' lineup had grown and become huge. I brought keyboardist Irwin Goldberg, aka Steve Gold, in from the Outcasts. We had the Jones trio, Irwin, myself, Jack Shaffer, Pat McGinley, and a guy named Bruce who was the second bass player who helped us out when Beau wasn't available. NUTS! Bruce was someone's friend, and a terrible bass player. We kept his amp turned off but it didn't really matter because almost everything was plugged into one Magnatone amp, anyway. As I really didn't know Bruce well, Rook recently reminded me of his entrance and exit.

Rook recalls, "Bruce came into the band because he had a really good microphone. Also, Bruce didn't actually leave the band, the band left him, and he wasn't happy about it. A chance for the band to play the Chief Halftown show at Dorney Park, an Allentown amusement park, came up while we were trying to tell Bruce we didn't really need him in the band. Chief Halftown was a Native American TV host who had a regional talent show. The solution was to take the Dorney Park show under the name of "Jonah and the Wails." Jonah is Rick's middle name. As fate would have it, Bruce happened to be at Dorney Park that day and was pretty irate that we had booked a gig without telling him. We lamely explained that this was a different band that just happened to have all the members of The Limits, except Bruce. That's the last I heard of him."

Fairly soon after Bruce's departure, Pat McGinley left. Pat's demise was hastened by the fact that his dad was a pretty volatile Irishman especially when drinking, which was often. One night, we were performing at a lawn party hosted by Mr. and Mrs. Jones, and McGinley Sr. showed up roaring drunk. He pulled Pat away from the party, saying his kid better not play with any "jewboys". I guess he meant me and Irwin.

Those of us who remained in the band were getting serious. The Limits, now myself, Irwin, Rook, Beau, Chris, and Jack, got down to regular rehearsing and lots of gigs. I quickly assumed the roles of player and manager and knew only two words: record contract.

I think growing up, seeing my dad become a successful businessman, made me want to know how to run a band and make it a business of sorts. One of our first gigs was at the Allentown Moose Lodge for a teen dance hosted by local DJ and friend, Jerry Deane. Jerry would later own a great under-21 nightclub, The Mod Mill.

There was something different about The Limits from the beginning. One look at our first Moose gig said it all. Irwin played a grand piano wearing a Mexican poncho and serape. Rook, Beau, and I sat on three carved African stools for quiet numbers, and I played a Caribbean steel pan drum for the solo on "Kansas City." Besides being pretty good garage rockers, we had an artsy vision. Later, we would have our own version of a psychedelic light show, even showing Julia Child cooking movies on our drum head.

Around this time circa 1966, Mr. and Mrs. Jones graciously donated their garage to The Limits. We cleaned, carpeted, and paneled the room, and had our very own rehearsal space. Over the next two years, we rehearsed, recorded, and had some great post-gig parties in the garage. At this time, however, we were all really straight-laced kids—no booze, no drugs—we were, literally, high on music.

More Support from the Grownups

It's here that I want to thank Jim Musselman. Mr. Musselman was the art teacher at William Allen High School. No, he was *the* art teacher at high school. A former boxer and military man, he was tough, no nonsense, and conservative. What a teacher, what an artist, what a dreamer! I was one of his students, as was future Limits' drummer, Ned Earley.

Mr. Musselman encouraged and fostered individuality, freedom, creativity, and basics. We would routinely arrive at school before classes and spend early mornings in the art room painting, drawing, or sculpting. He had high expectations, and we wanted to meet or exceed them. He also believed in courtesy, manners, and moral behavior. Jim Musselman supported our music, helping us design drumheads, stage props, and anything else we needed for The Limits. Mostly, however, Mr. Musselman taught us to believe in ourselves and our dreams. I still dabble as a cartoonist and potter but he nurtured a creative spark that is still burning strong in me some forty years later. Much like Uncle Elliot, Jim Musselman showed that one could survive and make a living doing something one loves.

By now, I knew I had to find a way to make music my life and my business. I never dreamed of all the twists, turns, roadblocks, and expressways that would lie ahead. Mr. Musselman has said that our class, the Class of '67, was the most creative he ever taught.

Club Scene and Queenie's Cubs

Allentown, and by extension the whole Lehigh Valley area which also includes the cities of Bethlehem and Easton, was an important radio market, and it had a great teen scene. The Lehigh Valley presented a good rock band with a lot of opportunities to play gigs. Clubs like The Mod Mill, Purple Owl, Mad Hatter, King Arthur's Court, and The Third Eye all catered to the under-twenty-one crowd with live bands.

Ken Bray, along with his wife, Ginny, owned and ran the Purple Owl. Ken, Ginny, and I have remained close spiritual and personal friends to this day. Ken is also a talented silver and goldsmith as well. The Owl was my favorite club to play. Basically, it was an open space converted clothing factory, as I recall. Ken had fashioned a mini-Fillmore type light show with liquid gels and pulsating colors…pretty far out for Allentown. Mostly local bands performed, but occasionally Ken would book talent traveling through the area.

One such band was the California Spectrum. Most of us, being from middle class backgrounds, and still in high school, hadn't really seen West Coast, acid-laced hippy jam bands. This was 1966, remember. Well, the Purple Owl rocked that night. The Spectrum was really a superb sounding band…great songs, great look and attitude. Turned out that they changed their name shortly thereafter to The West Coast Pop Art Experimental Band and released several wonderful trippy albums. The early Limits were so impressed that we covered two of their songs in our live show. Many people thought they were Limits' originals.

Ken was also a few years older than most of us, but he was married, and had his own businesses, so my folks didn't mind when I decided to go with him and a group of jewelry smiths to help sell jewelry at the Rock festival in Miami in 1968. We all piled in Ken's truck, loaded with rings, bracelets, amulets, some food and lots of pot. Suffice it to say that by the time we got to Virginia, we had smoked our way to oblivion, and remained cranky the rest of the trip. The festival, however, was the real trip. Music from the Doors to the Beach Boys, and even an appearance by Maharishi Mahesh Yogi, Transcendental Meditation's founder. I never made it to Woodstock, but we sure had a helluva great time in the warm Miami sun. I vaguely remember a girl climbing into my sleeping bag one night without any adolescent coaxing from me. What a life!!

I digress. Back to the pre-drug, mid-60's days in the Lehigh Valley.

The local colleges, Muhlenberg, Lehigh, and Lafayette, held regular frat parties that also provided chances to gig. Some of the frat parties were straight out of "Animal House". One frat party really was our rite of passage. Booked to play at Lafayette College in Easton, we arrived ready to do our normal repertoire. We were in for a surprise. Someone had neglected to tell us that we were going to back up this Amazon black female singer and her bleary-eyed sax player. She was "Queenie Lyons,"

For one very bluesy, soulful night, The Limits became her "Cubs." Shit, most of us had never been past Philly or New York, let alone Detroit or Memphis. Rookie recently reminded me that this Queenie gig was a really important step in learning to entertain an audience, not just perform our repertoire. Letting some of the drunk frat guys sing was, at first, an exciting ad lib and also probably one of the reasons none of us ever became serious drinkers to this day. Those frat guys were gross! However, photos from that night attest to the fact that the young Limits could funk it up pretty well.

During this time, I was already opposed to the Vietnam War. I was not a protester, rather I just thought the situation was against my beliefs, and also unwinnable. Like many other band guys, we wore surplus Army-Navy clothes and other assorted gear that would separate us from the regular high school crowd. Well, one night at a Lehigh University frat party, my clothes nearly got the shit beat out of us. We had finished playing, our amps soaked in beer with drunken frat guys singing "Louie, Louie," and "Twist and Shout". It seemed like the typical 60's frat gig and had that same vibe I alluded to at the Lafayette College Queenie Lyons gig.

We were packing our gear into our van, which belonged to Irwin's dad for his home construction business during the day. Mr. Goldberg used the van, an old bread truck, to haul lumber and building materials. On Friday afternoons, The Limits would clean the van, put in a shag carpet and some seats and—VOILA!—The Limitsmobile was ready to ride. The only problem was that the truck logo still said "Heimbach's Bread and Rolls" on the side, but we thought, hey, not a bad name for a mid-Sixties garage band, right?

As we piled the gear into the Heimbach's bread, rolls and lumber truck, some drunk jock boys started yelling at me in my army jacket, calling me "fag" and "commie." At first, we thought it was a joke. Then the frat boys descended *en masse*, fists flying. We threw ourselves into the van and hightailed it out of the Lehigh campus, back to our suburban houses, just in time for my mom to ask, "Did you boys have fun tonight?"

Meanwhile, back at record deal-land, I thought we were ready to record and make the big time. We had "Say It Again" from my uncle Elliot, and a really unique arrangement of the Dale Hawkins classic, "Suzie Q", utilizing call and response. In June of '65, local recording engineer Pete Helffrich unloaded mobile recording gear from his finned Cadillac and transformed Jones' formal library into a studio! I recall Beau playing upright bass while Pete had drummer Jack Shaffer remove his kick drum pedal! Either the kick drum sounded terrible, or Jack couldn't keep the beat. No matter, it wasn't a bad recording.

Certainly, enthusiastic and innocent, the vocals were a strong point. I think we had a fairly original sound. Armed with photos and acetates—we're talking stone age here, friends—I started sending copies to labels, expecting A&R guys to come flying to Pennsylvania Dutch land, contracts in hand. After all, I had done my homework. I had gone to the public library where I checked out music resource books. By today's standards, the choices were meager. I studied *Billboard* and *CashBox*, the music industry magazine bibles. I also learned about licensing a song from a publishing company and paying mechanicals to use the song in a pressing. Before I had even turned sixteen, I was calling major record labels, actually talking to A&R people, and alerting them to be on the lookout for the smash single from The Limits. I was so enthused and innocent, I thought they actually would be looking for my mailing. Meanwhile, a local DJ, Gene Kaye, who later managed and guided Jay & The Techniques to national fame with hits "Apples Peaches Pumpkin Pie" and "Keep the Ball Rollin'," arranged an audition for the Limits with producer Bob Finiz of Jamie Records. I knew Duane Eddy recorded for Jamie, as well as other charting artists. This meant we were going to a *real* studio in Philadelphia to cut some demos.

Well, Bob is dead, we never did get copies of the session, and our version of "24 Hours from Tulsa" didn't quite cut it. However, Gene Kaye also arranged for us to back up Roy Head who had a smash with "Treat Her Right". We were nervous, but we did a pretty good job rocking behind Roy's hit at Saylor's Lake Pavilion, a resort in the Pocono Mountains in Northeast Pennsylvania. We were sure we were headed for stardom. As fate would have it, I backed up Roy some thirty years later at a gig near Nashville.

Our next big chance was to write and record a jingle for a New York-based hamburger chain started by Irwin's uncle. Simon Sez burgers was going to be the next big thing. We wrote a pretty damn catchy song, complete with a dance. "Simon Sez move your feet. Simon Sez keep the beat" or something like that. We were teenage boys, which means we also had an alternative version that was more fun. "Simon Sez beat your meat." The Simon Sez jingle project never saw light of day. The hamburger company went out of business before it started, and the 1910 Fruitgum Company, an Ohio bubblegum rock group, charted nationally with their original, "Simon Sez".

Chapter 3

A Goddess and Graduation

By the end of 1966, we were one of the top local bands in Allentown. We shared that distinction with The Shillings, Johnny and the High Keys, Uproar, King's Ransom, and Dooley Invention, among others. The music that came out of the Lehigh Valley in the 1960's was notable enough that in the spring of 2005, Distortions Records in Philadelphia released a great collection of Allentown Sixties garage bands, "Allentown Anglophile."

I was still handling all the booking and publicity for The Limits, but we needed something more. We needed better talent. We were dissatisfied with Jack and heard that classmate Ned Earley had left The Shillings. The Shillings were practically big time. Manager Dale Schneck had gotten them a deal with a subsidiary of Mercury, and they had released several great singles including, "Lyin' and Tryin'," "Just for You, Baby," and the Jackie DeShannon-penned classic, "Children and Flowers." Well, Dale popped in with Ned on one arm and the older, smoother vocalist David Purcell on the other. David had the stage name "Adam...easily tempted", and the idea was for The Limits to do our regular show, and then have Adam come up and do a set backed by us. We incorporated both guys into the band as one smooth, polished unit, and by 1967 we had recorded a batch of tunes in Jones' garage which had become our full-time rehearsal and recording studio. Irwin produced great results considering we had crap equipment, and he was mixing, engineering, and playing keyboards simultaneously.

During this period, one rather amazing show really stands out. We were hired to play a Sweet Sixteen party for the daughter of Max Hess, founder of famed Hess Brothers Department Store based in Allentown. We had a great time and as we began to pack up, we were asked to stay and perform a private performance for Mr. Hess and a few of his close friends. Odd for sure, but we were gonna get paid a lot more money. As the several men in the audience got progressively more drunk, they demanded we play songs with dirty lyrics...beyond "see the girl with the red dress on" variety. We'd never compromise our artistic integrity...or would we? Here's a sample I clearly remember from that night sung to the tune of "You've Got to Hide Your Love Away".

"Here I stand,
cock in hand,
bash my balls
against the wall..."

I guess smut and farts always get a laugh, even at a refined garden party in West Allentown in 1966.

Beyond Allentown

We began traveling distances to perform including the New Jersey shore, Philadelphia, and beyond. In the summer of 1967, we were hired to do a show at a Jewish summer camp in the Catskills Mountain in New York State, Camp Ta-Go-La. Now, you might think the moniker is a Native American tribal name, but actually it stood for Tameroff, Goldberg, and Lapsky. As we were driving to the camp, we heard on Rook's Mustang radio, "A Whiter Shade of Pale" by Procol Harum for the first time. Fuckin' hell! It was maybe better than getting laid! We actually had to stop the car and listen, incredulously, to this amazing sound. To this day, this experience is burned deeply into my awareness as one of my musical highlights.

Was it good for you too?

The gig at the camp was fun. As we were older than most of the campers, they secluded us in the infirmary, but I think Dave Purcell got loose one night and might have gotten lucky with one of the princesses.

In 1967, I fell in love with a goddess, Candy Hunt. She was

my first and truest love I have ever known, and we went steady during high school. She and her sister and their friends were part of an amazing gang of kids that would attend every Limits show, and then all congregate at Jones' garage after a show. Me—the Jewish guitarist—had landed the ultimate *shiksa*. She was tall, blonde, and stacked.

What was amazing was that I had stolen her from Buddy Steckline, captain of the football team. Candy and I were genuinely in love, or we thought so. Buddy and the jocks were pissed. One Friday night, our friends were having a party, and all of us planned to go. At the last minute, The Limits landed a local gig, and once again fate faithfully intervened. During the party, Buddy and his football contingent stomped into the party house, trashing furniture and beating up kids randomly, looking for that "fuckin' jewboy guitar player." Rock n Roll saved my life! At my twentieth high school reunion in 1987, the original Limits reunited to perform and I ran into Mickey Mess, one of the jock warriors. We actually ended up laughing about the party incident. Candy and I are still great friends and she has a piece of my heart to this very day. Probably more than coincidentally, I was visiting with Candy and her husband and daughter at their home in the Virgin Islands when I got the call that my mom was terminally ill with pancreatic cancer. After the years passed, I imagine Candy was the right person to be with at that time. Her sister, Pammy, became the front cover model on the re-formed Limits' 1982 album, "High in the Mid-60's".

Irwin, Rook, and I graduated high school in 1967, and were getting ready for college. We had a five-night gig at The Mod Mill, thinking The Limits would end forever, but we surely were wrong! I didn't snag a record deal for the young band, but at seventeen I had made my way to A&R departments, learned about booking, performing rights, mechanical and synchronization royalties, and management responsibilities. That fall, I entered University of Pennsylvania in Philadelphia, Irwin attended Temple University also in Philadelphia (later transferring to Ithaca College) and Rook went to Gettysburg College about a hundred miles away. My mom, dad, sister, aunts, and uncles were all Penn grads, so I never gave another college much thought. Beau had enlisted in the military and wound up being stationed near Philadelphia. We kept the band together somehow during our freshman year, renaming it "Uncle Beau's Day Camp" reflecting the psychedelia and summer of love vibes.

During the early college years, we also recorded some really fine original songs. Fortunately, we have a pretty extensive library of early recordings, photos, and still movies. In the 2000's, we remastered and released a select group of recordings from 1965-68, "The Limits...The Earley Daze 1965-68". While I would continue full steam ahead in music, The Limits would lie dormant, only to resurrect in various forms, and ultimately reunite in original form decades later.

But in the meantime...

Cabbages and Kings

My first chemically-induced, mind-altering experience occurred in David Cohen's dorm room at Penn. I was a sophomore. The music was Quicksilver Messenger Service. The pot was good, I guess. It worked! Yes, Mr. Clinton, I inhaled. David, who later changed his last name to Kagan, recruited me to play guitar in a campus blues band, Mrs. Wigg's Cabbage Patch. It was short-lived, but pretty groovy. We played a gig in the U Penn quad for Parents' Weekend, pretty well electrified in all manners of speaking. My parents were shocked, as well. I was now sporting shoulder length hair and muttonchops. The band was really *loud*, and our bass player was wearing only a blanket and sandals. I was playing my first Les Paul guitar, and David was a dead ringer for a black-eyed raccoon with a huge afro. Hey, we were getting our higher education.

My childhood friend from Allentown, Bob Holtz, one of the Yocco's hot dog crowd, also attended Penn. Holtzie was incredibly straight-laced. He never once wore blue jeans. He was overprotected, very bright, yet beneath it all he had a riotous sense of humor.

He never got into the hippie/drug/politics thing, but our friendship transcended our opposite lifestyles. We remained close friends until his untimely, accidental death at age forty-nine. At Penn, Bob roomed with a short, red headed Jewish kid named Arnold J. Holland. Arnie was the kind of kid Dick Gutman and I would have mocked mercilessly in grade school. Always armed with an array of medicines for real or imagined maladies, Arnie was funny, intelligent, brusque, opinionated, and really, really loveable. He became one of the real inner circle of friends, sharing the peace, love, and everything else that went along with the Woodstock generation. Later, Arnie became a very successful entertainment attorney, and directed business affairs at several major record labels. Today, he is president of his own multifaceted entertainment company, Lightyear Entertainment. We are still the very best of friends, and I am convinced that our close association during the ensuing band years at Penn laid the groundwork for his career.

After playing all those silly frat parties with The Limits in high school, I could never have imagined myself rushing a fraternity at Penn. My dad and Uncle Elliot had been Penn Tau Epsilon Phi men, so I, along with Bob Holtz and Arnie Holland, joined the fraternity. It seems like TEP, with the exception of Bob Holtz, pretty quickly got the reputation for being the hippie frat house. Other than Bob and Arnie, there really are no other TEP guys I have stayed in touch with.

Candy had broken up with me after our first year at college. She attended Kutztown University about 50 miles away while I was at Penn. I was totally devastated when she broke up with me. She had been dating her ex-employer, Ed Russoli, and they subsequently got married. Emotionally, I was in a tailspin. Sex, drugs, and rock n roll became a needed escape, and maybe even a lifesaver.

Sometime over the next year, one of Philadelphia's finest rock bands emerged. At the time, the scene was ripe with Todd Rundgren's Nazz, American Dream, Edison Electric, Woody's Truck Stop, and others. After a brief incarnation with a female vocalist and flautist, Beau Jones and I teamed up with David Cohen aka Kagan and other Penn students Rob Hyman and Rick Chertoff to finalize the version of WAX. Local businessman Bill Sisca and genius/wacko John David Kalodner became our managers. My continuing and very close friendship and working relationship with internationally acclaimed entertainment attorney, Lloyd Zane Remick, also began during this time. Lloyd still, after 40 years, always makes time for personal and professional requests. He's a mensch and a powerhouse, too. I should be more like him!

If some of these names sound familiar to music buffs, it's no wonder. Some of the guys in and around WAX became huge in the music industry. John Kalodner was head of Columbia A&R in California for years working with the likes of Foreigner, Aerosmith, and many others. Rick Chertoff worked with Clive Davis at Arista, and became a successful and remarkable record producer, working with Cyndi Lauper, Joan Osborne, Sophie B Hawkins, and The Hooters. Rob Hyman, after disbanding WAX, would pair with another Penn lad, Eric Bazilian, to form Baby Grand, and later the multi-million selling 80's band, The Hooters. Rob and Eric also have enjoyed phenomenal songwriting success, with Rob penning Cindy Lauper's chart-topper "Time After Time," and Eric writing Joan Osborne's hit, "What if God Were One of Us".

Back to WAX. After several months of rehearsing on a daily basis, and yes, I mean seven rehearsals and writing sessions each week, we landed our first gig. One of our manager's friends knew a political candidate running for some local office. They thought it would be good publicity for him to have WAX perform live at a rally. The only problem was that there was no rally site. The solution was to have us perform on a flatbed truck going through the constituent neighborhoods. Saturday morning came, and we hauled our amps, drums, and PA on the flatbed, and hooked up to a gas generator. What we didn't know was that we'd be performing our hippie art rock music while driving through some of Philadelphia's toughest and poorest black neighborhoods. Well, we played loud and hard, and possibly gained a few fans, but had I been the campaign manager, I think a funky R&B band would have been a better choice. I don't remember if the candidate won or lost the election. I do know that WAX was rolling, and there was no stopping us. Within a year, we had performed with many legendary acts including John Mayall, Manfred Mann, The Everly Brothers, The Byrds, and more. Performing to over 25,000 kids at the first Earth Day festival at Fairmont Park in Philly, we could taste the stadiums to come, couldn't we?

The original Electric Factory, run by Larry Magid, was in its heyday at Twenty-second and Arch Streets in Philly, and WAX became one of the local faves. As our professionalism and showmanship improved, so did our fan base. Even when we weren't gigging, we had *carte blanche* access to the club. It was so great to be recognized and welcomed backstage to meet the likes of Derek and the Dominoes, Jeff Beck, Procol Harum, and others. I remember so vividly watching in amazement as The Who performed "Tommy", the rock opera, in its entirety. The Electric Factory was a club setting, not an arena. Just the four original Who members, surrounded by a wall of those British Hi-Watt amps, played this incredible music at ear splitting, earth shattering volume. It was beyond anything I had ever heard before or since.

I wanted this life more than anything.

We also had the opportunity to compose, perform, and record a soundtrack for an NFL Films special on the San Francisco 49ers Football Team. I haven't heard the soundtrack since we cut it, but I recall some great stuff. Our good friend and acid king, Dave "Cassidy" Capps, top local Philadelphia DJ, provided the voiceover for the program. We partied like crazy, played music all the time, and partied like crazy...wait...did I say that already? My childhood friend from Allentown, Bob "Westy" West, attended Temple University, and became WAX's equipment manager. Only one problem. He was *so* stoned all the time, the equipment was invariably set up incorrectly.

Downtown Philly was as colorful a place as you could imagine, filled with street people, hippies, professional people, and other assorted oddballs all coexisting peacefully. It is amazing we didn't get busted because the door at 1308 Rodman Street was usually open. Friends from Allentown would show up and end up staying for a while. Music and other stuff always filled the air. There was an old Russian woman who became the self-appointed block captain warning us against "praking cars" and partying till all hours. Tom, the old black parking lot attendant, was a phenomenal jazz and blues guitarist. He would stop by, and we spent many an hour jamming on the doorstep. David Cohen, WAX's vocalist and general good-natured soul, would bring a drunken wino in and feed him tuna sandwiches and milk. We'd clean up the puke afterwards. I wouldn't have traded all these experiences for anything.

Wait! How could we be a *bona fide* psychedelic rock band without the mandatory jail experience?

The Philadelphia Police were headed by the infamous Frank "Ratzo" Rizzo. Everyone knew he hated hippie longhairs and more than once we were rousted late at night, sometimes just walking downtown. Now, my memories aren't totally crystalline, but I sure do remember the night we got thrown in the paddy wagon. After performing at the original Electric Factory, Beau and his then-girlfriend Jill Martin, Arnie Holland, and I were walking back to the townhouse carrying guitars. There were probably a few other band guys and friends. Next thing we knew, a paddy wagon pulled up, loaded us in, and took us to a South Philly police station. We were probably stoned, but none of us recalls ever being told why we were hauled in. I do remember being scared in a stark police room, and being searched presumably for drugs. After a while, we were told to leave, and later Jill told us that she swallowed several pills. We didn't even have a joint with us but Jill was the heroine, probably keeping us all from being arrested. I hope she and Beau had a nice celebration that night.

All this musical excitement kept us pretty much out of the political arena. We did play several large anti-war rallies. One beautiful spring afternoon at the University of Pennsylvania, the student body spontaneously decided to stage an anti-war "be-in" in lieu of attending classes. Being an Ivy League, rather liberal school, most of the faculty probably thought this was a good idea. Several bands including WAX, Edison Electric, and Woody's Truck Stop set up to perform outside, and at some point, a guy appeared on the roof of the TEP fraternity and began throwing an endless supply of psychedelic pills down to the crowd. Who the hell knew what they were, but no one asked questions. Within a short time, the Penn campus was a trippy, hippy music experience. I'm not sure how much anti-war protesting took place, but I know that lots of pro-loving happened.

The Draft and My First Record

At this time, the military lottery system was in place. It was so surreal to watch someone on TV picking birthdates from a rolling drum. If your birthdate was chosen early in the lottery, you were going in! A bunch of us were watching the absurdity, even laughing. I stopped laughing when my birthday, November 1, came up number nineteen. Before it could even sink in, the phone rang. My mom was crying, as by now both she and my dad were against the war. My dad had fought in World War II, but now saw the futility of Vietnam. I was prepared to do whatever I needed to avoid being drafted, and with the help of a great network of anti-war doctors and psychiatrists, I was fortunate enough to get a psychological deferment from military service.

OOOO, it's gonna be on my permanent record. Well, at least I would finally have a record out! Wait! Stop the presses! On my twenty-first birthday, November 1, 1970 we did sign a real, cash involved, record contract. Legendary producer and songwriter, Bob Crewe (Four Seasons, Leslie Gore, Mitch Ryder) had his own label deal with Atlantic Records. Now you gotta understand, here were four middle class Penn guys, plus Beau who was now working at a high security missile base, stoned most of the time, but still rehearsing in the back of a shoe store almost nightly. In addition, we ran our own Italian Water Ice stand to make extra band money.

I think just about every band in this time that got to the point of serious music career goals also got into serious sex, drugs, and rock n roll. We partied, performed, and still managed to pass our college courses. Beau, miraculously, managed to defend the country! Bob Crewe had been told about WAX by Lloyd Remick, our attorney, and we had also been pitched by the high-profile Philadelphia disc jockey, Hy Lit. We were told that Bob wanted to see the band. One night while we were rehearsing in the back of the shoe store, Bob Crewe and his entourage parked their limo outside our shoe store/rehearsal studio, heard us, and offered us a deal on the spot.

We signed the deal, and our managers rented a huge apartment for us on East Sixty-first Street in New York City. We ran into fellow apartment dweller Dustin Hoffman several times. Even our professors at Penn helped us glide through classes during this time. It seemed like everyone was supporting WAX. It was a totally crazy time. We were running around New York, partying, not sleeping, and expecting to make a hit record. We were slated to record at the famous Record Plant. The day we started, The Who were in another studio within the complex. We were in heaven—or was it hell? David, our singer, got deathly ill, and needed several Dr. Feelgood shots to be able to sing. Beau had to commute by train from the military base in New Jersey, and was often too tired to be effective. In retrospect, the biggest mistake was that Bob Crewe allowed us to attempt to produce our own album. We thought we knew how to make records. We wanted to control our own sound. Shit! Why didn't we insist that Bob, who produced so many million sellers, guide our project? Things spun out of control. We were not capturing the creativity and sound of the band. We took a hiatus, and my taste of the big time soured quickly. Crewe's label went bankrupt, the tapes were never completed, and we never saw a dime. Later, Jay Proctor, who led Jay & The Techniques to two consecutive gold records, would tell me bigger horror stories in years to come.

Welcome to the record biz, lads.

We did manage an audition with another label in New York City and performed over sixty minutes of live music. Thinking we might have a record deal, we returned to Philadelphia, but shortly thereafter, the initial version of WAX disbanded. Frankly, I think we were all frustrated and chemically impaired to a degree that our sensibilities were not quite right. Rob and Rick Chertoff started another WAX, which later evolved to become the successful Philadelphia band, The Hooters. Almost forty years later, the original WAX crew all gathered together to listen to the May 1971 live studio session.

[In August of 2009, Beau was diagnosed with brain cancer. Sadly, Beau passed away on September 3, 2010. In an ironic way, his illness brought all the Wax guys back into close communication to the point that we remastered our last live session and released the project through our friend, Arnie Holland's record label.[3] Looking back to these formative years, I expanded my knowledge of the music business. My craftsmanship as a songwriter took quantum leaps. I also saw first-hand how most of the industry works; it chews you up and spits you out. I didn't know what I would do next, but I wanted to be responsible for my career or lack of one. As much I loved playing, I wanted to be in control and run the operations as much as possible.

---

3   The last live WAX session is available at www.lightyear.com/index2.html

Chapter 4

MCM's: Marriage and Mantra

I met Carlie Welsh during the declining days of WAX. She was from an old Philadelphia Chestnut Hill family, but for some reason worked as a waitress at Day's Deli in downtown Philly. We met, and she moved in the next day!

When the band broke up I was totally lost, an Ivy League grad without a clue what to do. Carlie and I bounced around for a few months between Allentown and Philadelphia. We even stopped seeing one another for a while but, at Christmas dinner 1971 at her family's home, I asked her to marry me. Possibly, I was encouraged especially after Stan, her wonderfully stewed dad, said, "Dickie my boy, it's time to shit or get off the pot." Old Philadelphia family daughters did not regularly marry Jewish boys, and it was no small feat arranging a pre-wedding luncheon at the Philadelphia Cricket Club! I never saw so much booze and so little food! Carlie and I married on New Year's Eve 1971.

I had a wife, but no band, no music, and no direction. I thought music school would be a great answer and enrolled at Berklee College of Music in Boston. I couldn't stand it. I was a rock n roll guy, not some slick sight-reading jazz wiz. I have come to love jazz, and play it regularly in St. Augustine now, but at the time I was not *that kind* of long hair. I ended up plunging into daily songwriting while Carlie worked as a secretary. After one brutal Boston winter, I realized that was enough for me. We moved back to Allentown.

Frustrated, I went to work at Strongwear Pants Co., my dad's clothing manufacturing business. I would quit and rejoin the family business several times during the next 10 to 12 years. My father was an absolute saint, putting up the prodigal son. I should have known I was not cut out for this business. This is the truth friends: I was learning to make pants from the ground up. On the first day, after marking a pattern in chalk onto the cloth, I took the heavy manual cutting shears and made my first cut. As I stood proudly to inspect my work, I was missing half my necktie!

Even while getting stoned and partying, I did manage to learn some solid business principles, which obviously prepared me to carve out a niche in the music business in later years.

Far and away, the most important lessons my dad taught me were integrity, honesty, and taking responsibility. One time one of our pattern makers mismarked an entire range of cloth for pants. The result was a small error in sizing. In reality, the finished garments probably could have passed through, but my dad insisted that we tell the customer, absorb the loss, and remake the garments at our expense. In the long run, the customer remained with us for years. More than once I heard my dad tell me, "When they spit in your face, pretend it's rain." I took that to mean that rejection and criticism are part of any business. If you cannot develop your own self-worth and esteem, independent of the market place, you'd best not be in the business world. I have passed that advice on through the years not only to my son, but to many other musicians, artists, and friends. Only you know if you are truly proud of your work and accomplishments. It's great if the world knows them, to be sure, but that's not usually the case.

I remember freaking out more than once, feeling miserable, not wanting to work in the factory. I quit, and we moved in with Carlie's parents. In August of 1972, walking in Chestnut Hill, we saw a sign for a lecture on Transcendental Meditation. Remember...The Beatles, Donovan, Beach Boys, Maharishi? I had heard a lecture a few years earlier but was obviously not ready. Carlie and I decided to begin meditating. The hardest part was stopping pot for two weeks prior to initiation. I guess a clear head was good to start the practice. I called Beau to tell him about this TM thing, and amazingly, he told me he was scheduled to begin the very same day as me and Carlie! The connection with Beau remained unbreakable and close until his death in 2010.

I can't say that life changed overnight, but within a few weeks we went to a party and got stoned. I couldn't believe it, but it was the worst feeling I ever had, and I had really, really, really loved to get high. That was the last time I used any drugs.

The Allentown connection was very strong, as lots of our friends had started meditating. For the next few years, music was put on the back burner as Carlie and I took several advanced courses in meditation. In 1974 we, along with Beau and Rook Jones and some other Allentown friends, went to Belgium for three months to become TM Teachers. There were some 1500 people from all over the globe, and the atmosphere was euphoric and sublime.

The schedule was rigorous between extended meditation, class lessons, and lectures. I became very good friends with legendary jazz flutist, Charles Lloyd. During the mid-1970s, TM was enormously popular with celebs like Mike Love of The Beach Boys, magician Doug Henning and football legend Joe Namath becoming practitioners and spokesmen. Beyond all the hype, the truth is TM works. I felt strong, calm, purposeful, expansive, and much less stressed. I still practice TM twice every day some forty years later. Interestingly, in 2006, the famous filmmaker David Lynch, a long-time meditator, formed the David Lynch Foundation to help put TM programs in schools for kids. Stress free education is the goal.

At the end of 1974, we were expecting our first child. During an advanced TM course in beautiful Weggis, Switzerland, Carlie started having problems. Being with Maharishi was very healing, but shortly after we returned home, Carlie had a miscarriage at eight and a half months. The stillborn girl was grossly deformed with water on the brain. Doctors said we were very lucky, as the child could have been born alive, and would have deteriorated over time. It was still a very emotional time for both of us in our early 20's, but I believe my regimen of meditation, running, and songwriting helped me get through. I recorded a beautiful tribute song titled "Rachel", a bit like

Lennon's "Imagine", and it hit home in a soft, healing way.

Not long after this, Carlie got pregnant again and was feeling great. We were back in Philadelphia teaching TM, and I was also working in a health food store. I was also writing songs regularly and became good friends with Phil Terry, a friendship that continues to this day. Phil was one of the original "Intruders", a great Philly soul act on Philadelphia International Records. Philly International had a powerhouse songwriting team in Kenny Gamble and Leon Huff who wrote and produced music known as the Sound of Philadelphia for the likes of Intruders, Stylistics, Delfonics, and Blue Notes. I became a regular fixture at their studios, writing songs with Phil and even getting a few published. The music business bug was biting again—REALLY HARD—but fatherhood was at hand!

Jonah Andrew Levy was born February 5, 1976 at 1:52 AM. What can I say about a man becoming a father to a son? I recall the Blood Sweat and Tears LP title "Child is the Father to the Man". It all suddenly made sense. Aquarian through and through, Jonah even as a baby, was amazingly settled, happy, and serene. For a short time, we remained in Chestnut Hill, and while we weren't making much money, Carlie and I were really joyful. She was near her family, and I was playing music with local guys, teaching TM, and becoming a more devoted and involved dad each day.

For the life of me, I don't know why, but when Jonah was born, I felt, in the core of my being, that fatherhood was complete for me. I knew there would be no more children. I certainly didn't know what life would have in store for me in a few years. The issue of having more children caused some tensions between Carlie and me, but we remained in a smooth relationship, and moved back to the Lehigh Valley.

Family Life in Allentown

Once again, my dad welcomed me back to the family business. This time with a wife, son, and house, I decided it was time to grow up. Frankly, I had my doubts I could do it. The upside was, of course, steady money, stability, vacations, and being the boss's son. One of the best perks was that several times a week Carlie would bring Jonah to the factory, and the three of us would go for lunch. The best part of the pants business for me was actually creating designs and learning to sew. I made Jonah the cutest trousers when he was a tot, although he probably felt foolish wearing velvet trousers around the neighborhood. Original Limits' singer Rook Jones also had a son, and we resumed a close friendship. One of the very positive things about being back in the Lehigh Valley was reconnecting with my high school buds.

Musically, I wasn't doing much, jamming here and there, and playing in some local bands. For a while it was fine, because I loved being a dad so much that not much else mattered. You know the times when everything seems smooth—nothing too exciting or trying for that matter. I hate shit like that! I always feel itchy when things get too comfy, and that usually means something is going to hit the fan. And hit the fan it did.

Chapter 5

Limits Reincarnated

Sometime in 1979, life presented one of those *gentle* challenges designed to test one's sanity, strength, reason, and emotions. Gentle? No way! Carlie wanted a divorce and left with virtually no notice. In short order, I became a single dad! By the time Jonah entered first grade, I was working in the family pants business, being a mother and father, trying to keep a spiritual balance, and really, really missing music. However, there was no way I was going to wear a tuxedo and play "Feelings"[4] in a wedding band.

Carlie quickly remarried the exact opposite of me. My successor was some cowboy, a tough fightin', hard drinkin' redneck kind of guy. The pairing with "Mr. Anti-TM" lasted less than a year and a half. Soon after, she, her mom, and aunt got involved in some weird offshoot of Santeria, and it became increasingly disturbing and frankly, totally insane over the years. She married a third time, had two kids, and at one point, I struggled to keep Jonah on track during this period of instability. It was a particularly difficult personal time for my little family, but it's sure good song material. Thankfully, over time, everyone is back on track, and we are all great, loving friends, and an extended family of sorts.

The universe, the great spirit, or whoever he, she, or it is—up, down, around and keeping the cosmos in motion enveloped me with blessings beyond belief. I just had to embrace and believe

---

4   Feelings was written and recorded Morris Albert. Albert released it as the title song on his hit album, and the song hit #2 on the Adult Contemporary Charts. It became a wedding band standard.

them. TM gave me the serenity to ride through it.

Jonah and I were living "The Courtship of Eddie's Father"[5] type life. It was fun, close, very loving, open, and liberal. We had a few pretty wacky housekeepers, including one who thought her dog was an angel from heaven, and another who took Jonah to the homeless shelter for lunches. Jonah and I began going to Nassau each year for a dad/lad vacation, and to this day, we are best friends, amazingly connected. Although he is now married, we talk every day.

Art of the Schmooze

One day I received a call from Pete Smoyer, a local musician and recording engineer. He was producing a band and asked me to lay down some guitar tracks. In the ensuing weeks, Pete and I discovered we had a very similar and strong affinity for British Invasion inspired pop. Within a short time, we had recruited original Limits bassist, Beau, and ex-Shillings drummer, Hub Willson, and we resurrected The Limits. Of course, my goal was the same: record deal. Except this time, we were going to write, perform, and produce our own album on our own label. A whole new adventure was about to begin.

Having access to a studio was a luxury beyond belief, and hence Luxury Records was born. We didn't think much about live performing at the time, but focused on writing short, hook-laden pop gems. I started to study the ins and outs of record distribution, independent promotion, manufacturing, and particularly saw the potential of new markets and tools... college radio and music videos.

"High in the Mid-60's", The Limits' first self-produced, full length LP was released on our own Luxury Records in 1982. It's a good pop album. Of course, we never reached stardom from that disc, or any other for that matter, but we got airplay on hundreds of college radio stations. We even made a kind of cheesy video featuring local high school cheerleaders. The song

---

5   The Courtship of Eddie's Father was a hit television series that ran from 1969 to 1972 about a widower father who was raising his young son alone, assisted by a housekeeper.

"Just Another Girl" was perfect for tantalizing innocence.

I headed to Epic Records' New York City office armed with playlists and tracking records looking for the still-elusive record deal. Ron Alexenburg was Epic's [A&R guy?]. He listened to our music and heard my well-reasoned presentation about our recent bump in activity on the college radio circuit.

After a few quiet minutes, Ron looked at me and said, "Nice job boys, but college radio doesn't mean much, probably never will."

Boy, was he wrong, and I was pissed. That was one time I kind of lost it.

"You're full of shit," I told him, and walked out of the office.

Somehow a young pop fan and independent record label owner in France heard The Limits. Raymond Debord wanted to release us in France, through the respected Celluloid label.

In 1983, "Teenage Bedrooms" was released in France with a fantastic cover photo of yet more teenage nymphs dressed in skimpy negligees, having a slumber party. Our drummer, Hub Willson, is also a professional photographer. He took the album cover shot in my sister's bedroom. My parents had not changed the room since my sister Judi had moved out, some twenty years earlier. I was very flattered a few years later when I was visiting a major label in the UK still looking for a record deal when the A&R guy pulled out this very LP from his personal collection, but still wouldn't sign us!

The disc was essentially the same material as "High in the Mid-60's" except we added a few new songs, including the very 80s-sounding "I'm Still A Boy." By now we also had promotional agreements with C.F. Martin guitars with its local factory in the Lehigh Valley and Fila sportswear. Those kinds of endorsements were pretty odd for a group not many people knew. Then again, I was getting quite adept at the art of the shmooz. I had seen time and again how the industry pros on the business side dismissed musicians as too artistic, not capable of handling or discussing business. I began to develop two musical personalities, both real but distinct. By day, I was the manager, record executive, promoter, who could discuss royalties, distribution, and promotion with clarity and confidence. By night, I was the rocking musician who could act like a perpetual hormonally-engorged teenager onstage—and sometimes off stage too.

The video for "I'm Still A Boy" was pretty cool, a bit more advanced than "Just Another Girl", and featured a seven-year-old Jonah, as a young version of me. The video received some national airplay here and in France. I went to Paris for a week and did several great interviews for radio and press. Shit, you would think I would have learned by now, but guess what? Raymond Debord was never to be heard from again, and the royalties from the sold-out pressing of over 2000 copies are still in someone's pocket, not ours!

Like a bull in a china shop, or probably more accurately, like Beavis slurping cappuccino, I was still frantic about landing a record deal, sometimes to the point of missing out on the fun. Thankfully, time has mellowed me, and also after seeing friends and some big, big stars left with nothing after deals, has helped me shift my paradigm. Maybe it's a rationalization, but I don't think so. I get to make records, make my living in music, and call all my own shots. I have come to realize it's not a bad life.

Wrestling and Rock n Roll in the Basement

In 1985, my entire life was shifting. The family clothing business had shut down, mostly due to outsourcing of the entire clothing manufacturing industry. Also, both my dad and I knew that I really didn't like the family business. I enrolled at Moravian College in Bethlehem, Pa., to earn a degree in Elementary Education. Some of the best few years of my life were just around the corner.

I got a job almost immediately teaching sixth grade at Nitschmann Middle School in Bethlehem. I think I became known as that cool teacher who also plays in a rock n roll band. I did play music in class, and really had a ball. I connected with the kids and felt like I was giving something back. I still mentor students to this day. Meanwhile, Hub and Pete Smoyer had grown tired of the pursuit of the deal, while Beau and I wanted to do more live performing.

The next few years were really exciting, as Beau and I brought various people into the band, and gigged regularly, mostly doing all our original stuff.

We played New York City a few times a month...places like Kenny's Castaways, The Bitter End, Trax, and even The Ritz. We also recorded our 1985 five-song EP at New York's Battery Sound Studios, produced by RCA staffer, Mike Getlin. Our great mate Pat Wallace added amazing guitar and vocal work to this incarnation of The Limits.

"Twin Girls," "Simple Life," and "Own the World" were huge productions, probably right for the time.

My house in Bethlehem was a potpourri of art, music and children. The doors were never locked, and all the neighborhood parents knew where their kids were. The basement was a combination band room and wrestling room complete with padding. Jonah and his buddies would play till all hours, and The Limits would rock out as well. I was way too committed and busy for a girlfriend, but a nice "seeing to," every once in a while, fit my schedule perfectly.

At the New Music Seminar in 1985 in New York, I met Tony Barwood, a manager from Liverpool UK. I was, naturally, pitching The Limits' latest effort, and Tony was managing Liverpool's "The Icicle Works" who were quite popular in Europe at the time. I gave Tony a cassette, and several weeks later got a call from him while his band was on tour in Canada. He *loved* the stuff. Right then we decided we would work together and have remained best friends for the past thirty years. I have been to England several times pitching music. Tony has come to the States, and our friendship is one of the great benefits of this business.

With the EP[6] entitled "VINGT" which is French for "20"-commemorating 20 years that Beau and I had been playing together, we approached music business legend Sid Bernstein.

---

6   EP=Extended play record is a term used for a record that has more than one single, but less than a full LP or long-play album that typically holds 10 or more songs.

Yep, that same Sid who promoted the Beatles at Shea Stadium, and managed—or maybe mismanaged—the Young Rascals.

Sid offered us a deal. He had a new label, New York Music Company, and our Luxury label was going to become a full-fledged subsidiary. Beau, my dad, and I had put money into the EP, and we were prepared to finance a small indie label. The opportunity to be a real label, sign other acts, and promote The Limits was exciting.

Why the hell do all my contacts go out of business? Good thing I kept my teaching gig, because soon after we worked out the details of the deal, Sid disappeared from the radar screen. The Limits and the Luxury record label were, as usual, fending for themselves again.

Chapter 6: RockRoots

RockRoots

Shortly after the Sid Bernstein experience, while I was still teaching, I developed the concept to have a rock band perform assemblies in schools teaching the History of Rock n Roll. I was always appalled at how dismally *square* most music classes were, especially in elementary and middle schools. I had very little formal training, but I learned so much playing in a band.

When I started teaching in the public school system, my friends assumed I was a music teacher. No way. First, I probably didn't know enough theory and fundamentals to formally teach. I hadn't spent that much time at Berklee to have absorbed enough theory to legitimately teach music or be certified as a music teacher. I can read chord charts, but still can't read those dots and lines. Secondly, most music teachers I had run across had no clue about the real world of gigging and making records. That's the world that excited me.

RockRoots was born in my brain.

RockRoots had very simple beginnings. The idea was to have a live band set up in the auditorium, complete with amps, drums, PA system, and trace the formative roots of American pop and rock n roll. The band would perform examples of early immigrant music, dances, rhythms, blues, country, big band, rockabilly, early rock and tracing it through modern music all while playing and interacting with the kids.

I discussed the concept with Beau and we knew a perfect artist to join us. We recruited local acoustic master and storyteller/singer Dave Fry, added a drummer, and RockRoots was born.

With my teaching experience, and Dave being a seasoned children's performer, we knew we would have to reach the kids immediately. Hit them with some loud rock n roll, then guide them on a journey that would unfold in both an entertaining and educational manner. We came up with songs from various eras and included stories and spots where kids could interact with us. It was a real challenge to fit several hundred years of musical traditions into a forty-five-minute assembly program. When we finally had a script and score, we debuted RockRoots at Nitschmann Middle School, where I was still a teacher, in 1986. The kids and staff went nuts! They loved the music, stories, interaction, and the staff all felt the program was really educational, and more importantly, needed in the schools.

During the next two years, while I taught at Nitschmann Middle, and Ironton Elementary, we performed RockRoots assemblies very sporadically when I could take a personal day off here and there. We knew we had something very, very viable and profitable, too.

Over thirty years later, Dave still performs RockRoots in schools in Pennsylvania, New Jersey, New York, and Connecticut. I put a RockRoots "South" together after moving to Florida and played in over 100 schools in the Sunshine State. Our early taping of a PBS program in Pennsylvania won us an award for "Best Single Children's Program." Since moving to Florida, I have produced six additional music education videos for kids, and now market them nationally via the best school and library catalogues. My business experience really paid off, as I was able to carve yet another niche for myself in the music business. I recently sold the video rights to a national educational materials company.

The Phone Call that Changes All

During the early RockRoots years, I was beginning to hazily formulate a plan to earn my living solely from music. A major piece of the pie turned out to be Apple, Peach, and Pumpkin Pie, and was soon to fall in place.

In 1986, Kenny Rodgers and other entertainers spearheaded

a huge national charity campaign, "Hands Across America" to relieve hunger and homelessness in America. In Allentown, a concert was planned featuring some local acts that had achieved varying degrees of success. The Shillings performed, as did The Cyrkle from Easton, PA. The Cyrkle had recorded "Red Rubber Ball," and "Turned Down Day". They were also the only American group managed by Beatles' manager, Brian Epstein. They, in fact, opened for the Beatles. However, the feature of the concert was Allentown's Jay & The Techniques who scored consecutive gold records with "Apples Peaches Pumpkin Pie" and "Keep the Ball Rollin". Several weeks after the benefit, I received a call from a friend telling me that Jay Proctor wanted to put a full-time band together and start touring again. Jay had been severely burned in a club arson fire in the early 70's. After difficult years, Jay was ready to return to the stage. The oldies market was resurfacing, and it seemed promising. However, I was teaching, doing RockRoots, and raising my son while still pursuing the Limits' dream. Jogging and TM filled out the rest of my daily routine. What more could I do?

Well, I went to a rehearsal with Jay held in the back of a bingo hall next to a strip club. I looked at the seedy surroundings and thought, "I guess some things never change." Then I heard a voice that was, and remains, simply amazing. Al Green, Otis Redding, and classic soul weaved together into Jay's unmistakable sound. I immediately committed to working with him. The band, however, left much to be desired. Job number one was to find suitable players, and over the past twenty-five years we have been fortunate to have had mostly quality players and genuinely nice guys. Original Limit Beau came along for this ride, too, and became our bassist. Within a matter of months, I was managing the group, and learning all I could about the nostalgia market, agencies, promoters, and venues. In short order, we were traveling around the country performing shows with many Fifties, Sixties and Seventies artists, many whom have become very close friends.

One of my key ideas was to have The Techniques' band be capable of backing other artists who did not carry their own full-time bands. This would enable a promoter to package a show for less expense, fewer musicians, hotel rooms, etc. To this day, The Techniques are well known for being a great backing band. One amazing story comes to mind. Several years ago, at a huge Fourth of July show, we were slated to perform and also back other acts on the bill including "The Miracles". Seeing four white guys on stage, The Miracles refused to perform, thinking we could not handle their brand of R&B. The promoter was beside herself, and Jay went into The Miracles' dressing room. He basically said to the guys that they should do a quick one-song rehearsal with his band, and if they weren't happy, then they shouldn't perform. Well, we totally kicked ass, and saved the show. Of course, we never got a thank you from either the act or the promoter. I guess if I got paid in "thank yous" from artists, agents, promoters, and even most musicians, I'd be struggling even more than I have for years! What...and quit show biz?

It was in 1987 that we first backed Peter "Herman" Noone, lead singer of Herman's Hermits, in Baton Rouge. If my time with Jay and The Techniques marks a turning point in my career, my time with Peter set me firmly on my new path. Peter and I have been friends ever since. For over two years I was his full-time lead guitarist and bandleader. More on that later.

On the Big Time Rock N Roll Road

Strange things always happen on the road. First, it's a total license for grown men to act like kids. Fortunately, we had all grown out of our drug-crazed days, and even the guys who drank would have only a couple of beers after a show, no binges and barfing. Even if we were calmer now, we were still a rock band traveling on the road, and that separated us from the workin' stiffs.

I surprised Jay and the entire band one fall. We were slated to do a twelve-city benefit tour for Police Benevolent Associations in Pennsylvania and Ohio. We have done many, many of these shows over the years. Some of the organizers have been less than scrupulous, but all in all the organizations benefit financially, and the local organizations get their money.

I sold my private car and bought a used 15-passenger Chevy van. Within a few days, I had the interior rigged to comfortably seat the band and carry our gear. I also had "Jay & The Techniques" stenciled on the sides, as well as the hit song titles. I vividly recall Jay's delighted amazement when I pulled up to his house to pick him up to start the tour.

Of course, in the music business, there is always a sleazeball or two or three or more lurking behind the scenes. We were booked to play a festival in Canada, near Niagara Falls. We arrived at the border in The Techniques-mobile, were treated well by the border patrol, and continued to our destination. When we got to the site, the promoter ran up to the van, excitedly saying, "Jay and The Techniques! Wow, what are you guys doing here?"

Looking confused, I said, "Well, we're booked here for the festival."

What actually happened was that some sleazy agent had sold the promoter on The Contours ("Do You Love Me?"), but booked us, telling neither party! I am sure the promoter paid more than our normal fee, and the agent pocketed a hefty sum. Fortunately, the show must go on, and Jay & The Techniques kicked ass playing the hits, and our classic soul renditions of Motown, Memphis, and Philly songs. The audience loved it but, musicians beware! This shit happens every day, so be ready for it!

Later, during a short southern tour, we got stiffed in one club, but gamely kept going.

Road Warriors Are Different than Us

Long time road warriors were different from those of us who had lived a quiet middle-class existence for most of our lives. I'll never forget going into keyboardist Wayne "Benny" Smith's hotel room to find him spraying his black pants with Lysol. Apparently, he brought only *one* pair of pants for the entire ten days!

In Chattanooga, I nearly ran off with a gorgeous brunette. She actually came up on stage and took her shirt off and we switched tops. Damn! At the last minute, I went back to the hotel with the guys instead of with whatever her name was. I guess I had grown up, despite my best efforts to the contrary.

Around this time, I met a promoter who would become a good friend. Ron Simpson promoted many events around the Atlanta area, and a big oldies show that was a huge annual event for Fox 97 Radio. My first big stadium show was at the old Fulton County Stadium in Atlanta. Jay and The Techniques were part of a huge bill that also featured Peter Noone, Frankie Valli, Dion, and several other acts. I have since played many huge outdoor shows, but the first time was amazing. Taking the stage and seeing fifty thousand people, well, all I can say is that for that time on stage, there was no difference between me and The Beatles, The Rolling Stones, or any of the other pop giants.

In the summer of 1988, I got a shot of cosmic courage! The Limits had become like a prizefighter who retires and comes back, retires and comes back. The Limits had just completed "summersessions 88", a group of songs that would become our latest final LP. For this record, which came to be titled "Close Enough for Government Work," Pete Smoyer came back on board as co-producer and engineer. Fantastic guitar work was added by our friend and temporary Limit, Roger Girke. Ron Vail, an absolutely brilliant singer, writer, and Brit-pop fan, gave Beau and I some perfect backing vocals. I would later recruit Ron to be one of Peter Noone's Herman's Hermits in 2000. Percussionist Wayne Achey rounded out the project. Certainly stripped down from 85's "Vingt," The Limits' "Close Enough for Government Work" is a great example of our blend of sophisticated garage rock and well-produced power pop. The music industry bible, *Billboard*, lauded the record as "combining nice garage scruffiness with 60s pop sensibilities." Shit...we did it again! Another fine album and no record deal. Luxury was getting known as a great no-hit label!

I also met and fell in love with Leiza Horonzy that summer. The Limits were playing at a local club, and she walked in with a girl I knew. Leiza was a traveling nurse scheduled for assignment in California. No way! Meeting Leiza, like meeting Carlie, happened quickly and decisively. Quite shortly later, she moved in. I had visited Nassau back in the Sixties, and after I became a single dad, Jonah and I visited there every year. In December 1991, Leiza and I got married in the Bahamas. I remember the license saying Leiza was a "spinster", meaning unmarried woman, in their colloquial vernacular. We divorced several years later but are still connected and loving friends.

Jonah spent the summer of '88 in Chicago with his mom and was set to return to start eighth grade in the fall. I had *no* job! My teaching assignment had ended because the lady I replaced had completed her pregnancy leave. Cosmic courage kicked in. I decided now or never—NOW! NOW!—I would forge a life in music.

I knew RockRoots could work, and I knew Jay & The Techniques could work. Could I make it all work without a steady paycheck and benefits while supporting myself, Jonah, a home and other expenses. Truthfully, I didn't give it much thought. I took the leap. Looking back, the best things I've ever accomplished have been intuitive, heart-driven leaps. Occasionally scarred and bruised to be sure, but it's the only way I know.

My education research led me to Young Audiences, a nationwide educational booking agency. They booked educational assembly programs into schools and had over thirty chapters nationally. In the Northeast, they had ample classical, jazz, dance, and theatre presentations, but nothing like RockRoots. Both the Philadelphia and Princeton, NJ chapters added us to their rosters. Soon, we were working much harder than rock musicians should work. Meeting at five or six AM, driving to Philly, or the coal regions in Northeastern Pennsylvania, or the New Jersey shore, we spread the gospel of pop music to gleeful kiddies. Of course, the one time we played at an all-girl Catholic high school was worth all the sunrise drives.

RockRoots had grown into a wonderful program, demonstrating so many influences, rhythms, instruments, and styles, while relating the economic, political, and social issues of the period.

By this time, Jonah, who had been a child actor and model,

was totally focused on becoming a Special Effects/Makeup Artist. For a few years, I had been schlepping him to New York City for modeling and film auditions. He did land a major magazine shoot and had several callbacks for major films. Twice he lost the roles to one Leonardo DiCaprio. They looked amazingly similar at twelve-to thirteen-years-old. Jonah realized that his real passion and talent were behind the scenes, specifically, special FX and makeup. I, of course, became the guinea pig as Jonah would pour alginate (mold goo) over my head to make life casts. Our kitchen oven was now used exclusively to bake prosthetic foam appliances. I was, and am, amazed at his talent, diligence, and expertise. I gave him total support, never once saying, "Make sure you have something to fall back on."

RockRoots and Jay & The Techniques were working fairly steadily. I was touring. Leiza, Jonah, and Scooter, the family hound, all got along famously. I expanded my public relations work, getting Jay some TV appearances and a deal to reissue his classic albums. My business instincts kicked in and I started to represent other oldies artists, some exclusively, some not. Great talents like Tommy Roe, Barbara Lewis, Dennis Yost, the Classics IV, Freddy Cannon, and others came under the Rick Levy Management banner. Remembering my Heimbach Bread and Rolls van days, I figured Jonah was probably a bit embarrassed when I would pick him up at school in my fifteen-passenger van emblazoned with "Jay & The Techniques" on the side.

All in all, it was a great time, but Allentown was too *(&^%$ cold. Warmer climates were calling.

Little Ricky age 3 "My destiny was cast" *no photocredit*

"Uncle" Elliot Wexler, my musical guardian angel and
inspiration no photo credit

The Limits 1967 (before the Summer of Love)
back row Irwin Goldberg, Rook Jones,
Chris Jones, Beau Jones
front Ned Earley, me in striped t-shirt
no photo credit

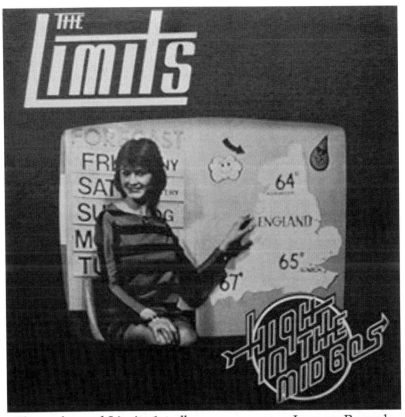

The re-formed Limits 1st album on our own Luxury Records
"High in the Mid 60s" (cover design Hub Willson)

WAX, Philadelphia original band from 1969-71
l to r David Kagan, Rob Hyman, Rick Chertoff, Beau Jones, me.
photo courtesy of John Kalodner

The Levy Clan c. 1982
Me, Myra (mom) Mort (dad), Judi (sis)
front Jonah (my son) Aren (Judi's daughter)

Jay Proctor
"lead singer of Jay & The Techniques"
I started my management/bandleader career w Jay & the Techniques
photo credit Hub Willson

Me and Peter Noone
"I was Herman's Hermits bandleader 2000-2002" *no credit*

© Hub Willson

TOMMY ROE and the band
at BB Kings in NYC. I brought Tommy out of
retirement in 2011. We have been great friends
for 30 years.
l to r Lee Brovitz, Mike Campbell, TOMMY, Mike Liddy, Me.
photo credit Hub Willson

THE BOX TOPS
founding members, Gary Talley, Bill Cunningham, along with me.
No photo credit

Me and son Jonah c 2013 at the Orlando Make Up Show. *no credit*

Chapter 7

Rockin' Florida

For some reason Jay & The Techniques had played Florida quite a bit. We moved among Orlando, Miami, Ft. Lauderdale, Gainesville, and Ft. Myers regularly and I really liked it. The weather was great, and I still felt fairly close to home. All the times I'd been out West, it was just too far and LA was way too surreal for me. Instead, of course, I could grow old and join all the other *yiddisha alta kakers* in Florida!

In the spring of 1991, we were booked for a week-long engagement at Wolfman Jack's, a fantastic oldies club in Kissimmee, Florida near Disney World in Orlando. It was a blast driving the big Jay & The Techniques van down I-95, having people honk and giving us the thumbs up sign during the entire trip. Jonah flew down to meet us, and during my off hours he and I scoped out the city and schools. We quickly made the decision that we would move after his junior year in high school, and he would complete high school in Orlando. We chose to live close to Dr. Phillips High School. They had a fabulous art and drama program. Jonah still returns to the high school to give classes in sculpture, and I have arranged several fundraising concerts for the art department. Like the old saying goes: imagine if they had a bake sale to raise money for bombs. Pisses me off! Art and music are so important for kids.

Leiza found a great apartment for us, and in the summer of 1993, we became Floridians.

I had no job, and few contacts, but the move just felt right. Within a month, I had struck a deal with Orange County Schools to get a grant to perform RockRoots in most of their elementary and middle schools. Only one problem, I had no band.

RockRoots Southern Expansion

Orlando is a hotbed for music and musicians, although much of the atmosphere is cookie cutter, commercial, and way too theme park for me but, the caliber of musicianship is very high. I soon recruited some great guys. I had met Paul Parker, a phenomenal drummer, at Wolfman Jack's, and he was interested in the educational program. He introduced me to a fine keyboard player, Steve Senkeiwicz aka The Senk. We found Louie Vigilante, a young bass player. Louie would later play bass for the Backstreet Boys. RockRoots South was ready to roll. For the next two years, RockRoots performed over 150 performances in and around the Orlando area. The response from students and faculty was just like up north. They loved it!

I also began a wonderful association with Dr. John Sinclair, the head of the music department at Rollins College in Winter Park. Winter Park is a gorgeous cobblestoned suburb of Orlando with trendy shops, beautiful homes, and a very upscale feel. Rollins is a beautiful college. With Dr. Sinclair's help, eventually I put together more programs for schools, and eventually developed my concept to produce a full line of music education videos for children.

My commitment to education became a profitable venture for me. Dr. Sinclair knew musicians from all over the Orlando area from jazz, classical, Latin, and Caribbean influences. Because I was familiar with the Young Audiences organization, I suggested that we develop our own smaller, but similar, educational program. Dr. Sinclair agreed, and we developed Fresh Starts, modeled after the Young Audiences concept. Besides continuing to perform with RockRoots, I oversaw the development of ensembles to perform in schools.

I worked with Dan Jordan, a brilliant jazz saxophonist and educator, to develop "Journey Through Jazz". Like RockRoots, the program traced the roots and rhythms of America's only indigenous musical form, Jazz.

I knew a program involving African music was vital for

school children. With the large number of African-American kids in the U.S., I thought an exploration of some of the black music roots and customs would be an enlightening experience. Margo Blake, a black dancer and storyteller, teamed with Dr. David Closson to develop "African Drumming and Dance". Complete with colorful costumes, drums, rhythm instruments, audience participation, stories, and songs, the "African Drumming and Dance" program has enjoyed tremendous success in the schools.

Already existing was a group of teachers who occasionally gave presentations about Renaissance music. Music teacher Stephen Nelson and his cohorts dressed in velvet Elizabethan costumes, played authentic instruments, and transported children back to Medieval times with their program, "Ars Antiqua-Sounds of a Distant Tyme".

Funny what a small world the music business is, and I found more Sixties hitmakers in my path. Tom Reynolds, a steel drum player and maker, was part of the 60's pop group, Hamilton, Joe Frank, and Reynolds, best known for the mega hit, "Don't Take Your Love Out on Me Baby". Tom and I had many mutual friends and acquaintances within the oldies market. With my suggestions and his expertise, he put together a fantastic program on Caribbean music. "Caribbean Carnival" features the music, instruments, and rhythms of the Caribbean countries. Tom also demonstrates how steel drums are made, played, and tuned.

With the huge Latino population in Florida and, more generally in America, I knew we needed a Latin music program. Chuck Archerd is a phenomenal bassist and accredited educator. He also had an existing Latin performance group. He was enthused to develop "Latin Legends". This exciting performance introduces kids to music such as rumba, mambo, cha-cha, songo, meringue, and salsa. Hard to keep the kids from getting up and dancing during this show!!

Finally, I recruited Dr. Sinclair himself to be moderator of a program entitled, "Every Note Counts-Instruments of the Orchestra". Featuring a live orchestra of both professional and student musicians, this program introduces students to the instruments of the orchestra, the various sections, and how they play together, much like a well-trained sports team.

Having seen the success of RockRoots, I began to formulate a plan to multiply the profitability and prestige of these unique programs. I would produce professional quality video presentations of the programs, complete with teacher study guides. Then I'd just sell them and make beaucoup bucks! Simple, right? The Rollins music department had a great facility, and I had a friend who was a very talented videographer.

Just as I studied the oldies market, I investigated the school and library catalogues, and any other ways of distributing the videos. The videos, now DVDs, are carried in many of the most prestigious school and library catalogues throughout the country. Interestingly, in this age of increasingly sophisticated technology, I purposely kept the Special FX editing to a minimum. I always featured a live student audience, and as a performer, I knew the selling hook would be the interaction between the students and musicians. Besides, kids get enough glitz, bells, and whistles with their own video games. I guess I could make this even bigger, but that would take more time from my first love of performing and playing music. However, I am very proud of the many, many letters and emails I receive with accolades from music teachers, social studies teachers, and librarians.

Finally, Full-Time Music Business Career

My activities as a manager and agent really took off, as I was now devoting full time energy to a career in music. I was already a good player, but always knew that far better players were around. My goal was to balance performing and writing along with building a successful business side. I don't think I could ever give up the performing side because it really balances me. I found great musicians locally in Florida to fill in as "Techniques" along with myself and Jay.

During a trip to Nashville, a new phase unfolded. We were taping a TV show at the old Union Station. In the audience was Gary Talley. We met, and I learned he was a session musician, songwriter, and former original guitarist for The Box Tops, who recorded chart toppers "The Letter," "Cry Like a Baby," "Soul Deep," and "Neon Rainbow." Gary said that the original members had been thinking of regrouping, including the mysteriously famous Alex Chilton. Alex had formed the band Big Star after The Box Tops and is generally considered the father of Alternative Rock. He has a huge cult following.

Along with Gary and Alex, there was Bill Cunningham (bass), Danny Smythe (drums), and John Evans (keys). They were planning to record an album in Memphis. I told him about my management company, activities, and told him I would love to work with the group. More importantly, I was a fan. The early Limits had always performed "The Letter" at all our shows. Another cosmic connection here: Gary told me that Jay and The Techniques was on the bill of the first show The Box Tops played outside of Memphis after "The Letter" was released. He said The Box Tops and Jay & The Techniques shared a makeshift stage atop a hot dog stand at some fair in Philadelphia.

What a business this is! I just love it.

A Bit About Phony Oldies Acts

I flew to Memphis at my expense and met the guys at the old Onyx Studios, home of the Bar-Kays. I spent a few days with them as they worked on "Tear Off", a great album of covers of songs that were important to each of them when they were kids. That Memphis started an association that continues to this day, and I have been representing The Original Box Tops since then. We also put a completely phony group calling themselves The Box Tops out of business. I am very active in trying to stop bogus acts with no original members from performing.

The short story is I have represented The Box Tops for fifteen years, and, tragically, this wonderful relationship ended on March 17, 2010, when legendary singer, Alex Chilton, passed away from a sudden heart attack. His passing is a great musical and personal loss. However, in January of 2016, founding members Bill Cunningham and Gary Talley, along with myself, put The Box Tops out on the road again, and are playing concerts all over the US and internationally as of this writing.

The proliferation of phony groups has really hurt the business in many ways. First, of course, fake acts usually work cheaper and therefore take work away from the original artist. Also, the public is cheated because the acts are usually billed under the same moniker as the original band—The Drifters, Coasters, etc. _ rather than "A tribute to such and such." I don't think any artist would oppose the tribute bands, but when women or men who were never part of the original group can earn money singing the acts' songs, and representing themselves as original, something must be done. I am not familiar enough with the trademark laws, but I believe if the name trademark lapsed, anyone can purchase it. Could you imagine a multitude of Beatles performing? All the Beatle tributes bands, Beatlemania, Fab Four, are clearly recognized as tribute bands. In the case of The Box Tops, the imposters were nothing more than a crappy lounge act who simply used the name fraudulently. Their final show was in Tennessee a number of years ago. The original Box Tops' members had done their homework and spent the money on proper legal representation. When the phony act announced, "We'd like to perform our #1 hit we recorded..." a federal marshal stopped the show. That was the end of the phony Box Tops.

Unfortunately, some acts have sold their name, and even when audiences see singers who could not have been born when the hits were big, they still watch the show instead of demanding their money back. There are several artist organizations now actively pursuing legal channels to change the laws and punish violators. Most of the Fifties and Sixties artists got screwed the first time around with shitty contracts. It would be great for them to at least have exclusivity to their own name!!!

An amazing, and often emotional, event has occurred with almost every Sixties artist I have worked with over the years. Even though most of the songs are pure pop, Top 40, and not necessarily gut-wrenching emotional works, I have seen many grown men cry at concerts. Why? Well, many of the songs came out during the Vietnam War era, and these same songs apparently evoke memories of the time. "The Letter" by The Box

Tops, is one of those songs about rekindled love, and I have seen vets talk to the band after a show, literally in tears. I remember a show with Jay & The Techniques in York, Pennsylvania, a city not far from Allentown, when a local Vietnam vet came up after the show, eyes filled with tears, thanking Jay for making a song that reminded him of his home area during the war. Some people dismiss the music as lightweight bubblegum, or whatever, but the visceral reactions by so many men and women are what keeps this music alive.

I am proud to be part of this ongoing tradition.

Jonah Graduates and Leaves Home

During this time, Jonah graduated high school and won scholarships to many art schools. None of them really taught special effects makeup. He took a course in Orlando at the Joe Blasco School, and then surprised me and Leiza by saying he was going to California. He'd arranged an internship with Optic Nerve, the special FX studio that did the work on the TV show *Babylon 5*. What could I say? I was scared, but I knew it was a great thing. Besides, his maternal grandmother lived in California at Newport Beach, and he would stay with her. It was really hard letting go, but I am glad I did. Jonah spent about six months in California, and really grew as an artist. He also learned first-hand about deadlines, quality work, and professional expectations. He then got a scholarship to the Art Institute of Chicago, a very prestigious art school. He started but was quickly unhappy with the courses.

"I'm tired of seeing kids dressed in black who can't even draw," he told me.

In Chicago, he met Chip Williams who became his makeup mentor and later best man at his wedding. Jonah went on to do the makeup for the Lyric Opera of Chicago. He would return to Orlando as a makeup artist for Universal Studios. He became lead make-up artist at Universal, and following his family business instincts, he also has his own Special FX company, Blue Whale Studios. Proud dad? You bet!

Life has been filled with cool associations for myself and

Jonah. In high school, Jonah was, and remains, really good friends with Joey Fatone from N'Sync. Before that group was formed, Joey and some kids would come to our apartment and sing doo-wop. Hmmm.......I wonder what would have happened if I got them before Lou Pearlman?

It was great having Jonah back, but I was now ready to fulfill a lifelong dream to live by the beach. I think I held that dream close ever since those childhood visits to Atlantic City with my parents, watching them swim in the moonlight! Leiza and I had visited St. Augustine several times, and from the first moment, I felt like I was at home. Leiza had real problems with the town as a place to live, and eventually this was a factor in our splitting up. We moved to St. Augustine in 1998, and I entered yet another childhood, buying a surfboard and really digging the beach lifestyle. When Leiza and I divorced, I bought a condo by the beach, and a new phase of music, management, and living began.

Om Shanti and Living in the Moment

One day in 1998, after a particularly frustrating day on my longboard—you know, approaching fifty one can get up, but not stay up as long!—I got a call from my friend Dennis Yost. Yostie was the original lead singer for the smooth Classics IV. They had such a cool, sexy sound with songs like "Spooky," "Stormy," and my fave, "Traces." He had a show in Hong Kong and needed a band. We would also back up some Drifters clone act. It was going to be a hell of a long flight for 2 days in Hong Kong, but I'd never been there, and the promoter met my budget request. For this gig, I needed guys who could sing as well as play. Frankly, Dennis is not as strong a singer as he used to be, and I was very concerned about the overall sound but I knew with good harmonies, we could pull the show off. I called Lee Brovitz in Naples, Florida. Lee was bassist/vocalist for Jay & The Techniques, as well as my business partner in Rick Levy Management. He's a great guy and has an impressive resume including working with The Shadows of Knight, and Cyndi Lauper. Lee recruited his friend Michael Junkrowski aka

Michael J for keys, and I pulled in Techniques' drummer Dave Ferrara. Besides being a wonderful drummer, Dave's a tattoo freak, pretty much covered from the waist up. I don't care to see down below. He knew of the famous Hong Kong tattoo studio, Ricky's, and was planning to have a full color dragon tattooed on his back. I said that if I ever got one, it would be cool to have it done in Hong Kong rather than downtown St. Augustine! I did get my one and only a small Sanskrit OM SHANTI symbol, and even that hurt. I don't know how Dave sat through his session, but the dragon is amazing!

Coincidentally, or maybe not, my amigo Peter Noone was on the same show. It was a riot to see a welcome sign for "Herman Shermits" at the venue. The show was great. It was held in the same hall where the British turned over control of Hong Kong to the Chinese. I guess our event was considerably less important, but still great fun hearing seven thousand Chinese singing along to all the oldies.

Herman's Hermits headlined, and as I walked around the room to get different vantage points, I couldn't help but notice—and object—to the overall sound. Peter, as usual, danced and pranced and sang his hits in top notch fashion. The band, however, sounded kind of like some version of .38 Special, too slow, heavy, ponderous. None of the light, lilting, British Invasion jangly guitar sound was there. Plus, they looked like Seventies arena rockers rather than lean, clean Carnaby Street lads.

Feeling that Peter and I had a good relationship and professional respect, I told him my opinion, and said I'd love to put a proper unit together for him sometime. He acknowledged some of the image and sound problems, but that was pretty much the end of it.

By the summer of '99, Leiza and I were separated, and it was delicate and painful but as my path continued to unfold, I knew it was the only choice. It's absolutely amazing how events, options, and decisions converged in a coordinated fashion.

I was promoting a series of lucrative shows in Winnipeg, Canada. Basically, I, along with the band, stayed in Canada and brought in different headliners over a month or so, including

Jay Proctor (Jay & The Techniques,) Tommy Roe, Freddy Cannon, and Barbara Lewis. Shortly after Jay's gig, he told me he'd been diagnosed with prostate cancer and would require surgery. He would go to Johns Hopkins in Baltimore to a world-famous surgeon and recover completely but, he couldn't work for months.

Now get this: Almost the same time Peter Noone contacted me wanting a fresh band just for a couple of cruises. I knew this was more than coincidence. I knew just the guys! Dave Ferrara, of course, and bassist Ken Bussiere, a total garage music and pop fanatic. I convinced Peter to let me add rhythm guitarist Ron Vail. Ron's a fantastic singer, and I knew he and I would really recreate the Hermit's sound.

Imagine! This was all thrown in my lap, all while I'm still reeling from a divorce, even though I instigated it. Also, I knew Jay would want to start performing as soon as possible. As in the past, I just made the leap, determined to live in the moment.

Chapter 8

Noone and Mourning

The band rehearsed in Canada and then back in Florida. Tony Barwood, my Liverpool pal, was visiting and helped out with vocals, as we sang backup in rehearsal. All these "Hermits" came from Allentown, Pennsylvania originally. Another amazing Allentown connection.

Other than me, the guys had never met Peter, and wouldn't until we got to the cruise ship. Well, we really went over the top. I had Sixties style British suits made and we even recreated the Herman's Hermits original drumhead logo. Peter was totally unprepared for what he saw and heard. We had become the Hermits...albeit grown up. Peter had a real band, a band that loved and honored his music, for the first time probably since his first go 'round with fame. He, of course, had stopped drinking years prior, so his energy, charisma, and voice were fantastic. The beginning days with the new Hermits were heady and euphoric. We entertained large crowds, fan clubs, and yeah, even groupies.

"They still throw underwear, it's just so much bigger now," Peter said.

In my two-plus years, we played almost a hundred shows each year, and I turned over the day to day operations of Jay & The Techniques to Lee Brovitz.

Ron Vail recently reminded me of what he considered the defining moment of our experience as the reconstituted Herman's Hermits. We had just finished shows on our third cruise ship our, the elegant Cunard Coronia. The band was celebrating in the bar. Now I'm not a drinker, maybe an occasional wine, but we toasted.

I looked at my Allentown pals and said, "Well, lads, we did it."

I know that I was pretty overcome with emotion to the point of a few tears. I realized that for over thirty years, I had been building and following a dream, and here I was, with my friends, performing with an icon, a legend…someone who was part of the music that restructured my DNA. We really, really loved this gig.

Ron halted the celebration.

"Rick, YOU did it," Ron said, alluding to my drive, passion, contacts, and pure love of the music and the business. I take tremendous pride and feel at the same time humbled by these achievements but know no other way of operating.

Now, dear readers, don't think I had gone completely soft and mushy in my middle age.

On that same lovely ship, I did manage to have a great romp with a twenty-six-year-old Polish cabin girl. As I come from a Polish/Russian background, how could she resist my charms? She even timed her holiday to coincide with our disembarking the ship in Miami and met me with a limousine to take us back to St. Augustine for some further adventures.

Be Careful What You Wish For

It really was tremendous fun in the early days with Peter. For a while, we operated like a real band and all hung out together. Within a few short months, however, I also realized that I was compromising my work ethic in this situation. Demands and expectations were changed on nearly a daily basis, and as bandleader, I was put in the middle of way too many personal issues. The truth is that Peter Noone's career needs are demanding and fluid. To think that we could really be part of a band consciousness was more idealistic fantasy than middle-aged reality.

Of course, all things come to an end. Peter and I are both Scorpios and thrive on control. I had some fantastic ideas for marketing and staging. Ron, with his background in TV production and set design, formulated some great ideas. In my heart of hearts, I know I could have made Herman's Hermits a more profitable operation, but the obstacles in terms of people and personalities on the sidelines prevented these goals from manifesting.

By 2002, it was obvious to both Peter and me that I should move on. First, I honestly didn't want to be on the road *that* much. Be careful what you wish for. I'd wanted to play with Peter for years, and experiencing it, I'm thrilled I did. I also realized I had evolved into much more than just a guitar player. With the Hermits, I couldn't utilize my management and promotional skills. Of course, I was consequently paid only as a sideman. Even so, I arranged a couple of small recording situations for Peter. Ron and Ken stayed on for a few more months, and Peter, in his usual fashion, changed things around to keep it fresh for him. As of now, Dave is the only member of my posse playing with the Hermits.

Peter and I are friends, staying in touch, and in February 2004, I guested with him at a show in Jacksonville. It was great being a Hermit for a few more minutes, but I also knew, in my heart of hearts, that our original unit was the best overall sound and look he's had since the original Sixties Hermits.

Within a month of leaving, I had arranged a forty-two-city tour for Jay and The Techniques, Freddy Cannon, and Merrilee Rush in 2003 to benefit firefighters nationally. I was so much more in my element. Jonah was also planning to marry in March of 2003. He was doing fabulously at Universal Studios in Orlando and taking on outside projects as well.

I had booked my other main act, The Box Tops, on a cruise in February 2003 along with The Buckinghams. I decided to tag along and just vacation and chill out. Again, as if fate pulled some loosely connected threads, a few days into the cruise we stopped in St. Thomas. I flew by seaplane to St. Croix to see my high school sweetie, Candy, and her husband, Ed, and daughter, Carla. Candy's sister, Pammy, and her son also lived there.

While there, my sister called. My mom's relatively minor stomach pains were diagnosed as terminal pancreatic cancer. Doctors gave her a week or two, at most. It felt right being close to Candy at that time, even though I had been married twice. For some reason, I felt strangely calm and accepting.

I flew home and the entire family converged at our

childhood house in Allentown. We spent some amazing final days with mom. She wanted to know all about Jonah's upcoming wedding. She wanted to make sure we cleaned dad's closets. She was concerned about everyone else being okay. She knew she would be perfect! That was mom, the peacemaker, love giver, harmonizer. Mom and I met one-on-one. She gave me her wedding ring. She praised me, above all, for being a great father, saying how proud she was of me and Jonah, and proud of how I followed my heart, doing what I loved. She also waited to pass away. Myra Demchick Levy died on February 6, 2003, one day after Jonah's twenty-seventh birthday.

Chapter 9

Limits Reunite

In the fall of 2003, I began to notice a real resurgence of retro pop music exemplified by short pop songs with a real edge. Also, some of the bands were distinctly low tech. I guess you could categorize it as "garage grown up". I loved Fountains of Wayne, and even high-profile bands like Strokes, Hives, etc. Although in my opinion, the genre was way better first time around but that's an old guy talking. Through my friend in Allentown, Bill Villa, a fine late-blooming pop writer/performer, I heard about a good record promo guy, Ray Paul who was also quite a power popster in his own right.

I decided to compile the best of the Limits 1980-1988 recordings into a CD. We had garnered some really strong reviews over the years, and it just seemed like a good idea. I realized we weren't going to hit the road, at least not without our Lipitor, Prozac, and—for some of the guys anyway!—Viagra.

Luxury Records reared its head again with the release of "Songs About Girls." I did a decent promo campaign with Ray and also with *New Music Weekly*, a publication that has filled the void left by the demise of *Cash Box*. To my delight, but not surprise, by early 2004, we were getting airplay on not only commercial AAA stations, but colleges as well. CMJ, the college radio bible, ranked us up there with some of their cutting-edge bands.

The CMJ review finished with the quote, "It's not about the hype, man. It's about the music!"

Eighteen and a Half Missing Minutes of Tape But Not Ours

Of course, I was also still handling Jay & The Techniques along with The Box Tops, and booking the nostalgia shows. We were actually presenting a stronger profile than ever before. One great show I produced, American Soul, featured Felix Cavaliere's Rascals, The Box Tops, and Jay & The Techniques with a special guest appearance by the Soul Survivors. We rocked the hell out of The Sands in Atlantic City!

In that same year, 2004, we also played at the Richard Nixon Library in California. WHAT?!? Yep, we backed our old buddy Tommy Roe. It was a gig to remember. I was so tempted to ask the curator where he stored the eighteen and a half minutes of tape.[7] In the midst of all the sound checks and jokes about the Nixon years, we got a call that Tommy and his wife, Josette, were in a terrible car accident on the interstate. Well, in my mind, Tommy Roe should be the spokesperson for Lexus. His brand-new Lexus was totally demolished except for the front passenger compartment, he and Josette made it to the gig, and we had a great show! A further reminder to love what you do because you never know what the next moment brings.

One day, I opened the mail to find a CD of a large group of early Limits' recordings. Irwin Goldberg, aka Steve Gold and The Limits' original keyboard guy, had remastered and finally put the stuff to CD. I listened to the CDs while sitting on my patio in St. Augustine looking out at the Atlantic Ocean. We really were a fun band. Oh, maybe we should get together and play again! By summer, I had brought up the idea to the guys, and it felt right to everybody. Rook, Beau, and Chris still lived in Allentown, as did Pete Smoyer and Hub Willson. Ned Early was in upstate NY, and Irwin was in Syracuse. Once we put

7   Richard Nixon's presidency ended abruptly in 1974 when he was impeached and left office in shame over what has become known as The Watergate Scandal. At the heart of the Watergate investigation was a question about a missing 18 and a half minutes of a taped conversation that was considered central to the investigation; the implication was that the section of tape had been erased by the president to delete evidence that would have convicted him. He was charged with obstruction of justice, among other violations, and was driven from office.

some thought into it, it just fell into place.

I had some space in my July calendar, and our pal and former Outcast, Mike Mittman, already had a steady Friday night oldies DJ gig at an Allentown nightclub, The Skybox. The owner was all for it. We had a venue. The local paper gave us a great write up, complete with my history, and including lots about the Sixties scene in the Lehigh Valley. My furtive little brain was cooking. In secrecy, I took the original Limits recordings to my friend's studio and put together a twenty-two-song CD, complete with cover, some liner notes, and titled it, "The Limits...The Earley Daze 1965-68", a play on Ned's last name, Earley. We set July 23, 2004 as the reunion date. Word started buzzing around, especially with internet buzz and through our classmates from high school. By two o'clock in the afternoon on July 23, people already were coming into The Skybox as we were setting up equipment. We had also invited members from other local bands from the era to sing and play with us. By our first show of the evening, there was a line outside, and it was packed inside. Dick Gutman, the block thrower, was there, as were many of our old friends and family people. Local DJ Jerry Deane, and Purple Owl club owner, Ken Bray, were there too. Rook took the mike, and I opened with the beginning guitar line of the Yardbirds' "Heartful of Soul."

The Limits were back just like at Jones' garage. It felt like we had only taken off for a long weekend. Over five hundred people attended the show at The Skybox. Jay Proctor of The Techniques made a guest appearance sounding great, as did members of Shillings, Dooley Invention, and High Keys. I have played thousands of shows in my lifetime, including large stadium shows, but I have never felt the surges of emotion as lifelong buddies rocked out in front of lifelong friends and family and sounded fucking great! They say you never forget your first one. Well, this was about as close to a visceral regression as I can imagine. We were all transported back to our teen years, band and audience alike, as we banged out songs like "Feel a Whole Lot Better," "Under My Thumb," "Last Time," "Light My Fire," and more.

A slow, but steady stream of emails started coming in from

Sixties fans, and some garage music websites. Several labels used our early tracks on their compilations.

We returned to The Skybox for New Year's Eve 2004, and all the guys have agreed to play some shows, festivals and the like, if the situation is right.

We are incredibly blessed that we have all remained friends over forty years, and very close friends at that. Every time I am in Allentown, I see the Jones boys, and am in constant touch with other friends from that era. Maybe I just live in the past, or maybe it just makes me feel good! Either way, I do know that those high school years with The Limits were unmatched in my life.

Chapter 10

My Rock & Roll Heaven

Like a kid in a candy store, I've lived in my own rock n roll heaven, and there are lots of stories to go with the journey.

You know these artists I have played for exclusively—Jay and The Techniques, Herman's Hermits' Peter Noone, and I manage and lead the band for rock pop pioneer Tommy Roe. Am I lucky? You bet your ass!

Here's a partial list of artists I have actually backed on stage over the years.

The Shirelles, Lee Andrews and The Hearts, The Tokens, The Angels, The Chiffons, The Classics IV, Frankie Avalon, Fabian, Lou Christie, Len Barry, Freda Payne, Andy Kim, Ron Dante, Bowzer, The Skyliners, The Beau Brummels, Bo Diddley, Danny and the Juniors, The Belmonts, Freddy Cannon, Tommy Roe, Merrilee Rush, Drifters, Coasters, Platters, Gary US Bonds, The Casinos, Chuck Jackson, Troy Shondell, Gene Chandler, The Chantels, Jimmy Clanton, The Miracles, The Contours, The Crystals, The Marvellettes, Spencer Davis, Joey Dee and Starlighters, Del Vikings, Diamonds, Dovells, Duprees, Frankie Ford, Sonny Geraci (Outsiders), Barbara Lewis, Chris Montez, Sam Moore (Sam & Dave), Randy & Rainbows, Martha Reeves and Vandellas, Mitch Ryder, Tommy Sands, Shadows of Knight, The Tymes, Maurice Williams...and more...

If I add the acts we've shared the stage with, I am humbled to the point of speechlessness! We've shared the bill with acts like The Turtles, Buckinghams, Temptations, Four Tops, Johnny Rivers, Badfinger, Beach Boys, Bobby Vee, Lovin Spoonful, Frankie Valli and Four Seasons, Trammps, Intruders,

Delfonics, Blue Notes, Mary Wilson, Stylistics, Jerry Lee Lewis, Little Richard, Chuck Berry, Felix Cavaliere's Rascals, Soul Survivors, Spinners, BJ Thomas, Lesley Gore, Fifth Dimension, Billy Joe Royal, Orleans, Box Tops, Sha Na Na, Monkees, Gary Puckett, Bobby Rydell, Paul Revere and Raiders, Mark Lindsay, The Searchers, Gerry and Pacemakers, Wayne Fontana-Mindbenders, Little Anthony, Billy J Kramer, Ripcords, Gary Lewis and Playboys, Tommy James and Shondells, and the list goes on and on.

In my heart and somewhere in my mind, I am still that little boy with cardboard sideburns. I can't believe I get to do this, and that I still have the hunger and passion to do it well. As 2009 came and went with a devastating economy, I may not have the money a corporate career may have provided, but I have tons of gigs, and I love the music, the people and the stories. Oh, if only the stages and dressing rooms could talk. Even though they can't, I can tell a few!

My Rock ŋ Roll Kiss ŋ Tell

Techniques' drummer Fred Domulot and I were sitting in a dressing room in Bay St. Louis, MS. We had finished several nights with Jay & Techniques, and the promoter asked us if the band would stay on and back Bo Diddley for two nights! DUH! That is like asking Bill Clinton if he wants another BJ from Monica. Bo turned out to be one of the nicest guys I ever met. I have been to his house, and we are good friends. Bo came in to change for the show, and Fred and I got up to leave, thinking he wanted some privacy. But Bo said stay and started talking and changing. Well, friends, at some point, he was down to his boxers, and Fred and I caught a view of why he should be called "The King." Whenever Fred and I want a laugh, we call each other and just say, "Bo's balls!"

There˷s a Kiŋd of Lush

Years before I joined Peter Noone full time, I would periodically get a call from his music director, Frank Annunziata, to have a band ready to back them on a show. I give Peter all the credit in the world for stopping drinking, because in his day, he was a gem! In Miami, we were playing at a big broadcaster's convention. The band was on stage and beginning the vamp for "I'm Into Something Good," Peter's opening song. Peter was nowhere in sight. Suddenly, Frankie, Peter's director told me to go next door to Mickey Rourke's bar and find Peter. I rushed over, and found him drinking, joking, schmoozing. I hustled him back to the venue, and without skipping a beat, we launched into a great show! He is a brilliant singer, entertainer, and could bring a crowd to its feet all by himself.

James Law

At the same Miami show, James Brown was the headliner. I was so excited to see him close up, that I nearly wet myself. James and his MC, Danny Ray, flew in, but sometime in the afternoon, a rickety old green school bus pulled up to the venue and no less than thirty-plus people piled out having driven overnight from Chicago. Rather than letting them rest, James called a rehearsal which went for some three hours. He probably was not happy from the show the night before. I sat with my pal keyboardist Steve Senk in the back of the club like two kids back at school, and watched a fucking *master* put his band through incredible paces, taking them to the point of absolute perfection. I have never forgotten this, and it's no wonder why James Brown is beyond a star. He is a quasar. His show that night was unbelievable.

Elvis, Jerry Lee, Ricky and Me

In Atlanta, we were doing a sound check at the GeorgiaDome for a big Fox 97 oldies show. I was jamming with my band, making sure the sound was right for Jay when I heard another guitar playing. I looked over and saw James Burton—yes, *that* James Burton—Elvis's guitarist, Ricky Nelson's guitarist, and now Jerry Lee Lewis' guitarist. I stopped, feeling very inadequate, and in the presence of genius.

James just smiled and said, "Keep jamming." We ended up playing for some twenty minutes...blues, funk, you name it. When he said I played really well, I felt I had arrived. A few years later, after a casino gig in Shreveport, Louisiana, we would all go to his club and jam until the wee hours.

Dirty Laundry

Jay and The Techniques were booked into a casino in Bumfuck, Iowa for New Year's Eve. We arrived the night before to hear The Drifters perform. Actually, this group was one of those batch of nameless, faceless imposters who still seem to proliferate the industry as the original band. They sounded good, probably because they were thirty years younger than the originals. Anyway, after the show, we went to their dressing room to say hi, and found them hastily taking off their sweaty, soaked suits and shirts and packing them into a box. Finding this odd, we asked what they were doing. Believe it or not, they were sending the clothes overnight to a group of "Coasters" scheduled to perform somewhere the following night. Shit, they could have at least sprayed them with Lysol!

David's Gests

It is December 8, 2004, and I have just returned from Memphis. On December 6, promoter David Gest (now deceased) threw an Extravaganza concert to benefit the poor of Memphis. Proceeds were going to feed them on Christmas day at numerous restaurants. David's a terrific and famous producer and promoter, and literally knows everyone in entertainment. He had recently moved to Memphis and wanted to give something back to the city.

He's also a fan of The Box Tops, Jay, and many others. So, on the sixth, I was sitting at rehearsal at the then-new Cannon Center for the Performing Arts, listening, in actual tears, to Billy Paul sing "Me and Mrs. Jones." What the hell am I doing here? But, I know. I am, in my own small way, part of this amazing fraternity. Last night was even more amazing, with a dinner and jam session with the likes of The Box Tops, Doobie Brothers, Gene Chandler, Jerry Butler, Petula Clark, and lots more, singing, dancing, being friends, and all egos all checked at the front door.

We all say the same thing, "I guess we do this till we can't!"

Never Felt so DIZZY

It's roasting in Temecula, California in August of 2005. My dear amigo Tommy Roe has asked me and The Techniques' band to back him at a private wedding reception. (Remember, I said I never wanted to play "Feelings" at a wedding!) It's so odd that the seemingly strangest gigs can turn out to be the best. We have always been one of Tommy's fave back up bands, and in fact, we really nail his hits accurately and nostalgically. We were told that the legendary genius of American Bandstand fame and subsequent host of New Year's Rockin' Eve, Dick Clark, was going to be there, as his personal assistant was the bride. I was also looking forward to seeing my old friend, Larry Klein, Dick's right hand man for years. As it turned out, Dick could not make it due to complications from his stroke earlier that year. We were performing the reception at a casino, so we assumed the room would be a showroom. Wrong! It was a very small meeting room/ballroom, and when we got all set up, it was like being transported back to the Sixties with small amps, small PA system, no monitors…just real *&^%ing rock n roll.

As we started rehearsal in the afternoon, this puckish, hippie-ish dude comes barreling in, maybe waiting to be impressed. It took me a few moments to realize it was Larry Klein. He had lost weight, looked just great, and whatever he was doing, I wanted some! This is the guy responsible for productions of American Music Awards, New Year's Rockin' Eve, and so much more.

The sound was so authentic and raw that Tommy and the whole band just smiled as we played "Sheila", "Jam Up Jelly Tight", "Everybody", and of course, "Dizzy".

Larry exploded, "Levy, you are a fucking genius. This music NEVER sounded more real!"

I feel proud and successful that I am part of keeping the honesty and integrity alive. So, maybe a nip and a tuck, and nap in the afternoon, and then do it all over again!

And Just Say NO!

Oh, boy! This little slice of rock n roll heaven actually happened in 1972. Now I loved to party as much as anyone... until I didn't. Back in the day, Carlie and I went to lots of concerts at Madison Square Garden in New York City. My ex brother-in-law ran the concerts at MSG. We saw Cream, Hendrix, Concert for Bangladesh, and more. On July 26, 1972, we saw the Rolling Stones, and it was Mick's twenty-ninth birthday. Through my brother-in-law, we were able to go to the St. Regis Hotel for Mick's party. Amongst the royalty were Muddy Waters, Bob Dylan, Woody Allen, Count Basie, and Zsa Zsa Gabor. I am somewhat ashamed and very sad to report that I have absolutely NO recollection of the party, nor riding in the elevator with my hero Keith Richards. My sister swears I did, and she did not indulge! So, if there is a moral, maybe sometimes "just say no" has its merits!

Chapter 11

Rick Levy's Highly Illogical, Largely Unplanned and, Frankly, Lucky Music Business Survival Manual

And now… for a light, yet down to earth, no bullshit point of view about surviving in the music business, with actual methods, tips, and attitudes…a must for musicians, artists, and probably any independent person!

First, you gotta love what you do. No shit! How often have you heard that? Have you really listened? LOVE WHAT YOU DO!!

One of those new age, self-help gurus said, "Love is an action verb." Well, future rock stars, she's right. You have to absolutely, unconditionally love your path. If music keeps you in wonder, in awe, in innocence, in childhood, you probably are well on your way.

Part of that love is remembering how you felt when it first clicked. I honestly can remember nearly every Limits' rehearsal and gig. Amazingly, and I have told this to many friends, I had a *bona fide* mystical experience (eg. no drugs) while playing at the Purple Owl in Allentown in 1966….an experience that involved losing awareness of time, space, and perception for a brief period, but still playing all the right notes. Years later, when I began the practice of Transcendental Meditation, and began experiencing pure awareness regularly, I knew that my music experience was the same state of total bliss and fullness. Now, that's really hard to package in a "How to Get a Record Deal" book, but for me, it's one of the key reasons why I can recall and reignite the love, passion, and energy every time I play.

I'm not a great believer in reading about playing music or studying manuals to become successful. For sure, there are some excellent reference books to guide both a novice and seasoned pro through the complexities of the business, but many "how to be a star" books are probably best used as paperweights.

That being said, let me divide the musical literary feast into three basic categories.

Memoirs

Memoirs. See? You're reading this! It resounds with your innermost core, right? I think the life stories about musical heroes are always inspiring. The meteoric rise and, oftentimes, the accompanying fall, is a valuable lesson in priorities and balance, or lack thereof. Invariably, behind all the money and fame is years of hard work and dedication. Besides, you usually get to see some cool pics of groupies and rockers in hot tubs.

Reference Books

Reference books are generally worth the cost. Books on the structure of the music business, contracts, royalties, licensing, publishing, and directories are vital if one wants to have some control and flexibility over his or her career. I also think the technical books on recording, home studios, demos, booking, and general business concepts are important tools that can save a musician lots of trial and error, time, and money.

How to Get A Record Deal

"How to Get a Deal" books...fuck 'em! Usually written by some wannabe who couldn't cut it as a musician. I find these books ridiculous. Granted, learning to communicate and present a package is important, but the truth is that there just ain't no way to guarantee a deal in this business. To paraphrase the 1992 Presidential candidate, Ross Perot, one needs to be a "road scholar", not a "Rhodes Scholar", especially in this crazy field.

You absolutely must learn by doing, not reading, not talking, not over-planning. It's the countless gigs, songwriting sessions, messed-up deals, heartbreaks, and joys that build your stamina, confidence, and eventual success.

Recently, Long John Higginbotham, my partner in The Falling Bones, and I were watching a young local band. These guys are all great players, but they've never been on the road or even strayed far from North Florida. As competent as the music was, it was also fairly lifeless. Long John turned to me and hit me with an unbelievable quote.

"These guys are just about three heartaches away from being a band!" Long John said.

You Can't Play It Safe

You can't become successful by reading about it and playing it safe. Success is as variable as musical styles. My definition is that I get up every day, blessed to do what I love. I make a living, but never stop striving and living to accomplish as much as I can.

To be sure, there are many normal jobs associated with the music industry. Radio, promotion, distribution, art, recording, and all the positions within record labels are basically corporate gigs that demand regular hours and fitting in the corporate scheme. The labels make it look like glitz and glamour, but it's a ladder up and down in every sense of the classic business models. If this is one's area of interest, my guide is definitely not for you!

Periodically, especially in slow times, I have envied the guys who have steady jobs, family life, and play on the weekends for fun. There is absolutely nothing wrong with this. Matter of fact, it's probably smart for most musicians. Music can be a totally fun process without financial pressures, disappointments and frustrations. What if it's in your blood?

What if the ebb and flow of "being what you do" and "doing what you are" are overwhelming, unmistakable, and unavoidable. I can only speak from personal experience and, as stated in the birth of this journey, I haven't arrived, but I haven't faded away either. Even during times when I held other jobs and had various responsibilities, I always managed to amass skills and knowledge I instinctively knew would be put to use in the music field. I never doubted, albeit sometimes on a subconscious level, that music was, and would always be, foremost in my life. That's vital to fellow pickers and bangers!

For me, knowing what I didn't want to do was just as important as improving in my areas of interest. Because the music and the bonds of friendship and brotherhood were so strong in the early Limits' years, I wanted to always have strong personal relationships with the people I worked with whenever possible. Growing up in the concept of a band, I really never felt, and still do not feel, comfortable in solo situations.

I alluded to the standard music phobia of ending up playing "Feelings" in a tuxedo, and for me that was equally nauseating to ending up playing "Free Bird" in smoky bars. I am not being aloof, or in any way putting down any other types of players, but that life was not what I wanted. I knew I had skills that could be put to use to try to build a career and still play the kinds of music that I loved.

I also never had any real interest nor technical skills in terms of engineering, amp design, or the like but, I always could hear in my head what I wanted. In studio situations, to me, the ideal team exists when the artist and/or producer can convey to the engineer the sounds desired. For sure, many artists are successful producers and engineers, but this skill area was not a strong point, so I did not put much emphasis on it.

I did, however, realize that I have very strong communication and people skills. I naturally gravitated to leadership positions. I have always been happier and more productive when I could utilize my management and promotional skills along with whatever musical talent I possessed. So, I would definitely encourage aspiring career musicians to explore related areas where they have an interest. I know guys who make a great living repairing amps and guitars and play full time. My long-time friend, Bob Birk, a successful booking agent, is also a very, very fine working guitarist. Because the value of education was drilled into me at a young age, I was able to combine music and education in developing my full-scale line of videos and DVDs.

You get the point by now. You can work in a fast food joint and play in a bar, living in mom's basement at thirty-four, or maybe stretch yourself, reach further than you thought possible, and advance. If you fall, get up and keep on truckin'! There *is* no endpoint.

As I've matured and gotten older, I realize more and more the value of balance and other interests. I find nothing more boring than hearing musicians talk shop all the time—about deals that almost were, gigs, chicks—imagine how their girlfriends feel! I have found that by developing other interests and even hobbies, my awareness expands, and that can be put to use in my music. I have been a runner for many years, and recently took up Yoga seriously. I feel and possibly look better than I ever have and have a more even view of life and the business. I also love to make pottery on a wheel, and while still an amateur, I started teaching a beginner class to a group of blind and visually impaired kids at the Florida School for the Deaf and Blind which is Ray Charles' alma mater.

I've alluded to my support of education, and to that end, I have been a mentor to students for the past dozen years. Giving back in terms of time, energy, talent, and sometimes money is a gift that keeps growing. Sounds corny, but I don't worry about myself as much!

Finally, practice humility. Nobody wants to hear you wag your tongue about how great you are or how amazing your band is. The music will speak for itself. To be sure, don't shy away from promoting your efforts, but do it with an attitude of gratitude as opposed to some ego-stroking bravado.

At the outset, I said this was a pretty unstructured manual for survival and progress in the music field. As I reread it, it makes pretty much sense! Maybe it's an unstructured manual for survival and progress in life, too. I believe I have come to follow most of my own advice, and only fall on my face periodically, but it sure as hell still happens. However, it's much easier now, and in fact, fun, to get up and start where I left off.

It's a trip!

Epilogue

Retire? Hell No!

The past decade has been nothing short of amazing. Going from my fifties into my sixties, this is a time in life when most normal folks think of winding down their careers and enjoying retirement in Florida. Wait, I already live by the beach in Florida. I have become busier, more creative and productive than ever. Thank you, Universe!

So much has happened in the past ten or so years. I thought I'd have had a published book much earlier with an epilogue that reviewed my life and events but LIFE has exploded on many levels.

On the personal front, Jonah got married and I became a grandpapa for the first time in 2006. My grandson, Brayden Sky Levy was born August 6, 2006. A beautiful girl, Leighton Harlow, came along later. Of course, I still refer to myself as the "terminally teen rockin' yogi granpapa". Jonah ended up divorced, but he has found his life's mate with Crystal. They have two beautiful girls… Olivia Grace, and Avery. In 2006, I also released a CD called "The Bushwhackers", a satirical country music CD targeting the Bush administration. It was picked up for worldwide distribution by my pal Arnie Holland's Lightyear label.

I was also quite busy with my local band, The Falling Bones, building us into the area's most popular Sixties party band. We released another CD and perform about a hundred shows each year.

Aside from all this, the oldies business has really slowed down, with golden oldies radio stations leaving the marketplace daily; the demographic is getting too old, and they (we) are not rampant consumers, which means less advertising revenue. The music, I believe, is as popular as ever, and will always be the "classic" high water mark of pop music and rock n roll. So as totally whacky as it sounds, many of the popular recording groups of the era are now playing dates at adult fifty-five-plus communities all over the country. It's become a very lucrative market. Retirees now still want to rock, not hear some schlocky borscht belt comedian. Part of my time is spent investigating this new potential market.

In my never-ending quest for "teenage psyche," I took on portraying my hero, Keith Richards, in a well-known Rolling Stones tribute band, Sticky Fingers ™. This was a short-lived and fun excursion, but ultimately not something I felt comfortable with.

One of the recurring themes in my life is striving for some kind of balance. Being involved in yoga, Transcendental Meditation, vegetarianism, and the lifestyle is a way to help not only slow down the aging process but keep me grounded to a more silent core of life. To that end, I finally plunged with dedication back into making pottery on the wheel.

I also am involved with the David Lynch Foundation. David is a famous film director (*Eraserhead, Mulholland Drive, Twin Peaks*) and is very committed to the TM practice. His foundation of Consciousness-Based Education aims to bring meditation programs to schools, especially in at-risk areas. The Foundation also teaches TM to veterans with PTSD and has had formidable results, helping vets renew, heal, and move on in their lives. I am very proud to be part of this great work.

So, the journey literally continues. I went to Fairfield, Iowa, home of Maharishi University of Management, for a David Lynch Foundation symposium. My trek for spiritual growth has taken me to various places, but I keep returning for short periods of intense silence and order to Fairfield. Yes, even in the deep transcendent field, I am, to quote David, "catching the Big Fish." Donovan, the legendary Sixties folk /rock singer is also involved with TM, and I am, in my active moments, planting seeds to possibly work with him in the future.

Don't count The Limits out yet either. I just put out a DVD compilation of ten videos from our indie "Luxury Records" label days during the Eighties. "Good Songs...Bad Hair" captures that post-punk, new wave era of creativity where Beau Jones, Pete Smoyer, Hub Willson, and I recorded some remarkable music.

Probably the most confounding and, at the same time, exhilarating overall experiences are how music and my relationship to it has come full circle. At this particular time, with our economic uncertainties, rising prices, home foreclosures, and a general psychological malaise, my particular niche in the music business has taken a huge hit. While the top echelon oldies acts are working fairly regularly, the smaller two- and three-hit artists that I've managed and performed with are struggling like never before. I've had to shift my awareness, perspective, time, and energy into making my local band into a somewhat profitable venture, not just mere sideline fun.

Then, an odd thing happened on the way to my bank loan. I totally love giggin' in clubs and entertaining people on the small scale. Don't get me wrong, I'm maintaining visibility nationally, but for the first time in many years I am having to watch every dime, and, in fact, do worry about it. The bright side, of course, is I am home more, can see Jonah and the family more, and can focus on meditation, yoga, swimming, and pottery. When I remain "present and thankful" with an "attitude of gratitude," I realize that music and performing is why I am here, and I must honor this regardless of the external rewards, successes or disappointments. This is precisely the journey being the success that I have written about and tried to live. Seemingly, it never ends. I encourage aspiring musicians and artists to examine their determination and passion throughout their careers. What could be more fitting than in summer 2008, my primal mates, The Limits, came to St Augustine for a series of concerts. Talk about literally returning to the well and coming full circle.

On April 30, 2008, my dad, Mort the Sport, passed away at 90. As Judi and I emotionally went through our childhood home in Allentown, preparing to sell it, I realized that being orphaned at any age is monumental.

The next couple of years were fairly normal for me, even given the waves I am used to. As I've said before, when life has become a bit dull and flat—WHAM!—something is coming.

In March, 2010, with the oldies business still dragging, we lost a great legendary talent. Alex Chilton of The Box Tops and Big Star died suddenly of a heart attack. From a management perspective, I lost a potentially profitable act, but I'd also lost a good friend. The band folded and I figured that was the end of The Box Tops. But wait!

Without question, the most emotional time in my life was about to unfold. My closest friend, Beau Jones, was diagnosed with brain cancer in 2009. As if the Lord of Karma him/herself stepped in, Rob Hyman of WAX found a reel to reel tape, forty years old, of the very last live in-studio recording session made by WAX. What transpired over the next few months, as Beau bravely, fearlessly, and even comically faced death, was the greatest expression and experience of love, friendship, reunion, and unity I have ever lived through. We re-mastered the WAX session, and again through Lightyear Entertainment, released "WAX...Melted" worldwide in late September 2010. Sadly, Beau passed away on September 3, before the release, but he resonates in our hearts all the time. The CD, by the way, earned great reviews, including Rolling Stone Magazine. Later that fall, we held Beaufest, a musical celebration of life. The Limits, Jay Proctor, Dave Fry, and yes, WAX performed. Eric Bazilian, Rob's partner in the Hooters, played Beau's bass lines superbly, and for twenty minutes the magic of WAX that went unheard for forty years, was alive and well.

In 2011, I was determined to keep the great Sixties music alive and wasn't about to let some great artists fall by the wayside. I kept bugging Tommy Roe, who retired in 2007, to perform. After many, many calls, he agreed to try a few dates. We got the gang together, Lee Brovitz, Mike Campbell, and Mike Liddy, and had a blast. As of now, Tommy is still making fans DIZZY!

I started playing in the Sixties, and now I am in my sixties, and not bored at all. I still love it. I live a beautiful life on the beach, maintaining health and balance, but always yearn for more. That's the nature of being in human form.

2014 was a stellar year. I was given the Lifetime Achievement Award by the Lehigh Valley Music Award Association, and also the Pennsylvania Governor's Award for Music. At a ceremony at the Musikfest Café in Bethlehem, The Limits banged out our time-honored garage rock, and I felt very honored to be so recognized by my home town area, even though I have not lived there for over twenty years. Without The Limits, I would not have had a career in music.

To be honest, that paled in comparison to August 2014, when Tommy Roe headlined International Beatle Week in Liverpool, England. He and I performed at the legendary Cavern Club on Matthew Street where The Beatles first performed, and I even got to do a solo set backed by my mates, The Shakers. Talk about a bucket list to cross off! I did it!

Have I done enough? It's never enough if you love what you are doing. Recently I opened a small pottery gallery in my home, and make sure I keep learning and growing in this expression.

Now, at sixty-eight, I am so very proud that after discussions and rehearsals with Bill Cunningham and Gary Talley, the original founding members of The Box Tops, I am managing and performing with this legendary Memphis blue-eyed soul group. The shows are honest, true to form, fun, relevant, and the group is getting popular again.

The renaissance has been overwhelming. In a short time, The Box Tops have performed on cruises, in casinos, and were a feature act on 2017's Happy Together Tour, covering forty-eight cities. In 2018 we performed on a German television special, and on November 1, 2018, The Box Tops were inducted into the Memphis Music Hall of Fame. Even though not a founding member, I am humbled to share the honor and join the legendary legacy of the Memphis Hall that includes Elvis, Jerry Lee, Carl Perkins, BB King, Otis Redding, Aretha, and more. Being partly responsible, along with the band mates and booking agency, for rebuilding such an important name in rock music is something I take seriously, but also delight in that I can kick ass on stage.

Lest you think I've attained the lofty enlightened state, I am working on it. I am also the neurotic schlub who battles impatience, limited outer success, some loneliness, aging, and writer's block. Of course, the huge difference is that I don't try to numb myself to these transient experiences. If I've learned anything, it is to embrace, recognize, and accept the shortcomings, yet be aware that I am so much more.

So, I gotta go now. I REALLY need to hear a loud E chord.

Before we sign off, though, the last word goes to that enigmatic LIMIT, best friend and extraordinary companion, Beau Jones. As this book was in its earliest form, Beau contributed his unique and intelligent perspective on our rock n roll life. His memoir is a glimpse into this very gentle soul's heart and mind.

Here's Beau.

Reflections on Rick Levy's Book

It's All About the Music

Well, actually, it's also all about the friendships! Rick Levy and I met through music, but we have developed a friendship that goes beyond, yet still includes, "the music."

Years earlier, in the 1950s and early 1960s, before I knew Rick, I had originally feared that "rock-n-roll" music was music created by delinquents, for delinquents—but, alas, I loved the stuff. Almost all the kids that I knew loved it. After all, it wasn't classical or "serious'" music, so how could it be any good. Parents hated it (actually, mine liked it; they liked all sorts of music, including the music my brothers and I and our friends were listening to).

In late1963/early 1964, when I first encountered the Beatles phenomenon, I, again, loved the music. On the dust-jacket of the 45 rpm double-sided hits "I Wanna Hold Your Hand" b/w "I Saw Her Standing There" there were a couple of early publicity shots of the group, consisting of two great black & white, posed portraits in which stood or sat four interesting-looking guys wearing unusual, collarless jackets and sporting outrageous (for those days) "pudding basin" haircuts; and who was that delinquent-looking, almost slow-looking guy in the bottom right of the picture on the "I Wanna Hold Your Hand" side of the record sleeve? He looked almost backward. Or, perhaps he looked like a ruffian or a sociopath to me. I must admit that he scared me a little! So, just as I feared—some more dumb rock-n-roll by some more dumb guys for us dumb listeners—damn!

(But their music sounded so great!)

I later determined that the person in question in the picture was one John Lennon. As they say, pictures can be deceiving, and I soon came to realize that I had been looking at the face of an arguable genius. Heck, he was probably mugging for the camera when the picture was taken. Looking at that picture again today, I'd say that all four of them were having a great time mugging for the camera when those pictures were taken and I now see the photos differently. In any event, here we had four bright fellows, John, Paul, George, and Ringo, along with their bright associates, Brian Epstein, George Martin, etc., putting out more great rock-n-roll music for us kids to hear. The Beatles! They played it, they sang it, they wrote it—and it was good! Maybe rock-n-roll music wasn't just by and for delinquents. Maybe it never was. Maybe it wasn't so bad after all. Maybe it was a legitimate activity. Maybe it would be ok to further pursue listening to and—whoa, yeah!—even trying to perform and eventually write pop music...Yikes!

In the spring of 1965, in Allentown, Pennsylvania, in what we here call the greater Lehigh Valley (USA, North American Continent, Western Hemisphere, Planet Earth, star system of Sol, Milky Way Galaxy, Local Cluster, This Universe—and modern physics now says there may be untold numbers of universes—etc.), a happy young group of fellows between the ages of fourteen and eighteen started gathering together and talking together and meeting and playing together to form a "rock & roll" band—a "combo" as we often liked to jokingly call it. My brothers, Rook and Chris; our new friends Jack Shaffer, Pat McGinley, Bruce Ehmer, Irwin Goldberg, and Rick Levy; and I started working up songs and started "playing gigs."

We had all formerly had some formal music lessons (from a smattering to over a decade's worth), usually on instruments other than what we were now playing (fortunately, instrumental skills are somewhat transferable), had sung in choirs, and had listened to and loved popular music on the AM radio, on vinyl records, and on TV.

During these times, we often ran everything through one or two strained amplifiers; we engaged other young bands in "battle-of-the-bands" competitions that were held from time to time in our Lehigh Valley; we recorded some tunes; we bought (or our parents bought) and sold and talked about instruments and amps and microphones (and maybe girls, too—talked about, that is, not bought or sold); we tried our hands at songwriting; we continued to get better at what we were doing; and we made new friends as new kids tried out for positions in the band, as we became friends with kids in other bands, and as new kids (and old friends) came to hear our band practicing and playing out.

Rick, in addition to being a very talented musician, had a good music business sense and plenty of drive, which helped to keep the Limits moving forward. To see Rick and my brothers and Irwin and Jack and the rest of them so earnestly engaged in pursuing the music and the other band activities quickly dispelled any misgivings I might have harbored that this band stuff was a frivolous endeavor meant for delinquents. These were good kids—bright, motivated, from "good" families; therefore, I felt that it was perfectly acceptable to participate, with some impunity, in this band project. We were not out to destroy the universe or to land in jail. We were out to play music and that was good, because I really wanted to be in the band. We have since speculated that our being involved in music had probably served to help to keep us out of trouble in our younger days because so much of our time was devoted to purposeful activity that we all loved, leaving little time or inclination to go totally off-course.

Through the ensuing decades, Rick and I have continued to develop our friendship, and have continued to be involved in music in one way or another. Rick is full-time and successfully wears many hats including singer/songwriter, lead (that's pronounced "leed," not "led," folks) guitarist, live performer, manager of a number of internationally well-known bands, etc.

Over the years, Rick and I have worked together in The Limits; Uncle Beau's Day Camp; WAX; a duet act that played in restaurants; a new version or two of The Limits; national recording act Jay & The Techniques; RockRoots©, with its educational and entertaining school shows; "sitting in" with various musical friends; backing up many big-name acts (on our tours with Jay Proctor); and so on. Even now, although I am not a full-timer in music, from time to time, Rick and I will get together and do some music. Whether it's gigging with Jay & The Techniques, or a Limits reunion, or songwriting, or just picking up a couple of guitars on the spur of the moment and strumming and singing a few songs in the living room, we have a great time.

Although Rick and I may approach some aspects of this whole music thing in different—albeit complimentary—ways, I think that we both appreciate a good "hook," that is, a catchy tune. In fact, that may be the main idea in pop music—a catchy phrase of music with just the right chords (and some good harmonies never hurt), maybe a nifty instrumental riff, and, if possible, some new, wild sound or effect on the instruments. We both like it and we both like to try to write it, sometimes together (I've spent many enjoyable and stimulating times writing tunes with Rick) and sometimes apart. I think that songwriting is one of the most fulfilling activities in the universe, and I believe Rick feels the same way about that. When the creative juices are flowing, you can nearly forget to eat and sleep because you can get so caught up in the song-writing process. You continually come up with musical "Eureka!" moments. Next, you might be stumped for a few moments. Then you solve a musical problem or two and you have some more musical "ah-hah!" experiences. When you eventually piece it all together and think and feel it through, you have a song! Then, it's over to a tape recorder or off to a recording studio or something to get the song into a "final" form for folks to enjoy. That entire process is, doubtless, its own greatest reward. Next to that, Rick and I have often stated, the biggest musical thrill would be to hear a generically re-recorded, almost sterile version of one of your own songs coming out of the speakers of an elevator or a supermarket somewhere. That would be better than a Grammy©.

Almost as good as songwriting (and recording in the studio) is playing out, live, before an audience. Rick and I have shared this type of experience innumerable times, from playing packed college fraternity/sorority houses in the 1960s with The Limits, to playing filled stadiums with Jay & The Techniques more recently, and it's still a thrill to this day. It's almost like what I imagine it to be like when you're in a crack combat team going into battle (without all the dangers attendant thereto): you're behind the curtain and you can hear the crowd, restless in its anticipation, like an opposing army, on the other side. Your band mates and you cast knowing glances at each other, all around, acknowledging what is soon to occur. Is everything ready? You all have trained and practiced for the mission at hand and you're poised and ready for action, even knowing that no two gigs are ever quite alike and that no gig is totally predictable. Each member fills a slot. Each position—singers, guitars, drums, bass, keyboards, dancers, castanets—is ready to work and blend and mesh together into a cohesive unit. Any nervousness that you might be feeling is less than the realization that the team can do this thing, and just adds to the energy that will be available for the show, anyway. Then, the MC gives the band an introduction, the curtains part, the count-in begins, and the music starts—the "battle" is on. If it goes well, the crowd loves it and is pleasantly "conquered" by the performance, no serious casualties, but just some happy concert-goers and a happy band and maybe a few new friends in the deal. Otherwise, it could be airborne tomatoes, launched rotten eggs, and smashed guitars!

Happily, what I have come to realize is that many of the people in the rock-n-roll/pop music business are intelligent, creative, interesting, funny, and even, as often as not, nice people. Rick is certainly one of those, and for that, I am glad to have him as a dear friend and an intelligent, creative, musical associate through the years.

Beau Jones
Allentown, PA

About the Author

Rick Levy is an internationally known musician, manager and tour manager. His career started in the early 1960's in Allentown, Pa., with The Limits. He went on to receive a BA in Sociology from University of Pennsylvania, and an Elementary Education Certification from Moravian College.

From 1985 until the present, he has been manager and/or bandleader for such notable pop rock artists as Herman's Hermits, Tommy Roe, Freddy Cannon, Jay & the Techniques, The Tokens, Bo Diddley, and currently is manager/guitarist w Memphis legends THE BOX TOPS.

Rick is also a professional ceramic artist, potter with his own "Glazed and Confused" pottery studio in St. Augustine, Florida, where he resides.

His son, Jonah, is sought after special effects makeup artist based in Atlanta, Georgia. He is co-owner of Blue Whale Studios.

Curious about other Crossroad Press books?
Stop by our site:
http://store.crossroadpress.com
We offer quality writing
in digital, audio, and print formats.

Enter the code FIRSTBOOK
to get 20% off your first order from our store!
Stop by today!

16501771R00066

Made in the USA
Lexington, KY
16 November 2018